FANCY FRETWORK

FANCY

The Great Jazz Guitarists

Leslie Gourse

THE Art OF Jazz

FRANKLIN WATTS

A Division of Grolier Publishing

New York London Hong Kong Sydney

Danbury, Connecticut

FRETWORK

This book is in memory of Sydney Jane Gourse and
Maureen Percelay Zusy, Harry Andrew Gourse and Norman Gourse.

The author would especially like to thank guitarist, composer, and teacher
Peter Leitch for his invaluable guidance in the organization of this book
and his insights into jazz guitar history and individual musicians.

Visit Franklin Watts on the Internet at: http://publishing.grolier.com

Book Design by John D. Sparks

Photographs©: Archive Photos: 71 (Blank Archives), 31, 66 , 73 (Frank Driggs Collection),
79 (Metronome), 111 (Joseph A. Rosen), 92 (Janet Sommer), 27, 62; Corbis-Bettmann: 56
(Frank Driggs), 12, 35, 89; Frank Driggs Collection: 9, 39, 41, 67, 86; Globe Photos: 127 (Lisa
Rose), 119 (Robert Roth); Lee Tanner: 100; Raymond Ross Photography: 49, 69, 82, 97, 114;
Retna Ltd./Camera Press Ltd: 20 (Larry Busacca), 123 (Andy Freeberg), 53 (W. P. Gottlieb),
70, 77 (Gene Martin), 65, 68, 104, 109 (David Redfern).

Library of Congress Cataloging-in-Publication Data

Gourse, Leslie.
Fancy fretwork : the great jazz guitarists / by Leslie Gourse.
p. cm. — (The art of jazz)
Includes bibliographical references and index.
Summary: Traces the evolution of the guitar in jazz history and profiles the world's greatest
jazz guitarists from the early 1900s to the present.
ISBN: 0-531-11565-8 (lib. bdg.) 0-531-16404-7 (pbk.)
1. Guitarists—United States—Biography—Juvenile literature. 2. Jazz musicians—United
States—Biography—Juvenile literature. 3. Jazz—History and criticism—Juvenile literature.
[1. Guitarists. 2. Musicians. 3. Jazz—History and criticism.] I. Title. II. Series: Gourse,
Leslie. Art of Jazz.

ML3929.G665 1999
787.87'165'09—dc2198-40014

CIP
AC MN

CONTENTS

CHAPTER ONE

The Types of Guitars and the Evolution of the Guitar in Jazz History

Of all the instruments, the guitar is the most popular. It can have a pleasant, romantic sound. Its tone blends well with the human voice — an important feature for any guitarist who sings or accompanies a singer. It has a wide range of notes and serves excellently as a lead instrument in a group, and it can also be played solo. A player can easily carry it around. So the guitar has many charms.

Prospective buyers may become confused by the variety of guitars on the market. The two main types are the acoustic guitar, which is not amplified—though it can be, and the electric guitar. Each of those two main categories breaks down into others.

The acoustic guitar breaks down into nylon- and steel-string guitars. These guitars are designed differently so that they can withstand the different types of stress that the strings place on them. Nylon strings place less stress on an instrument and produce a softer, mellower sound. Classical players use nylon-string, unamplified guitars and play them without a plectrum, or pick. Most jazz players usually play steel-string, amplified acoustic guitars, though occasionally they use nylon-string instruments to great effect. Steel strings have a brighter, louder sound.

The electric guitar breaks down into two main types: the solid-body and the hollow-body guitars. Traditionally, jazz guitarists use hollow-body instruments, while rock musicians play solid-body guitars. A solid-body guitar is made from a solid slab of wood, with electronics built into it, and with no body resonance, and it has a neck. The hollow body is more complicated and more difficult to build. First of all, it's hollow inside; it has a top, a bottom, a back, and sides, just as a bass fiddle does. Jazz guitarists usually prefer the rich sound of the hollow-body guitar.

While rock musicians normally use solid-body guitars and jazz players select hollow-body ones, musicians have been crossing over lately. Some rock musicians are using hollow-body instruments, while some jazz players select solid-body guitars.

But it's still traditional for jazz players to use hollow-body instruments, because the goals in jazz playing differ greatly from those in rock—particularly in terms of sound. And the music that jazz and rock guitarists play places different requirements on the instruments. Rock musicians must play loudly. And they can't play loudly enough on a hollow-body instrument, or they would have a problem with feedback—an electrical phenomenon that sounds peculiar, rather like a microphone booming. Of course a solid-body guitar can't produce tonal nuances. But those nuances are not so important in rock music. In jazz, they are paramount.

To be absolutely clear, the hollow-body guitars that jazz players use are called electric guitars, because they are amplified; in fact they are amplified acoustic guitars. The amplified acoustic guitar is primarily the guitar that we'll be referring to—though we'll also mention other types of guitars, as we discuss some of the great jazz players who have varied from the current norm.

For example, in the 1920s, Chicago musician Eddie Condon played a four-string guitar in the Chicago version of New Orleans or Dixieland

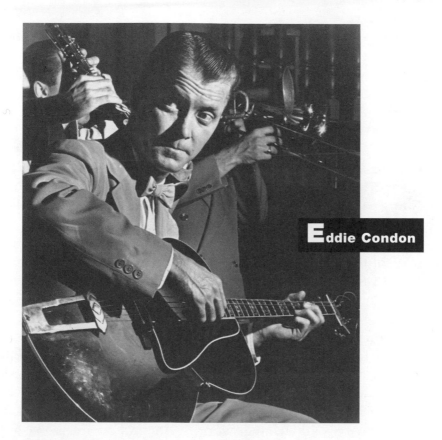

Eddie Condon

music. That type of guitar was an eccentricity. Used for rhythm playing, it has disappeared from the scene today. The four-string guitar didn't have the range of a six-string guitar. However, a very fine guitarist named Tiny Grimes, who played in the trio of Art Tatum—one of the greatest jazz pianists in history—played wonderful solos on a four-string guitar. (Of course, Art Tatum completely dominated his group and overshadowed his bassist and guitarist.)

The guitar evolved centuries ago from the lute in Spain. The lute was a pear-shaped instrument with eleven strings stretched along a fretted neck. Frets are markings on the lute—and the guitar—that guide a player to the right notes. Today, a guitar traditionally has six strings, though lately some jazz guitarists have been using a seven-string guitar, which has an extra bass string. That's especially helpful for a guitarist playing in a group without a bassist.

George Van Eps invented the seven-string guitar in the 1930s. As an old man in his eighties, he made four recordings with Howard Alden, a fine young jazz guitarist, in the 1990s. Van Eps was not especially important as a jazz player, but he developed technical books and a harmonic system for the guitar in the 1930s and 1940s. Many jazz guitarists have studied his concepts—the important systems of fingerboard harmony that he worked out on the instrument.

Guitar strings are tuned in the following way: E-A-D-G-B-E, with the thickest strings for the lowest notes. One of the best ways guitarists have devised to tune up their instruments is by use of an E tuning fork, an item sold in any shop dealing with guitars. Once a guitarist tunes an instrument with an E tuning fork, the other instrumentalists can tune up their instruments to the guitar.

It would seem from its size, and all the known elements of its musical capacities, and the frets on its fingerboard, that a guitar would be a relatively easy instrument to learn to play. But nothing could be further from the truth for jazz players. It's one of the most complicated instruments, particularly for modern jazz players. They must learn an enormous number of chords that rock players don't have to know. And jazz guitarists must also develop great dexterity and technical mastery.

"The human body was not built to play guitar," says Peter Leitch, one of the great, mainstream modernists of the last twenty-five years. "For one thing, a different set of muscles in each hand does different things. And if a guitarist practices too much, he or she could develop hand or wrist problems."

One of the first challenges is getting used to the steel strings, which can at first be hard on the fingers. But guitarists can use a plectrum or pick on steel strings. And that's the least of the challenges. Any book that teaches a person how to play guitar soon makes it clear that it can take years for a person to master the elements of creditable guitar playing. A student must find the right notes on the fingerboard, play chords, and make notes sound flowing and beautiful in the long lines that have characterized the art of jazz guitar since the late 1930s.

One of the first jazz guitarists was Brock Mumford, who played in the New Orleans group led by legendary trumpeter Buddy Bolden. Neither Bolden nor Mumford ever recorded, but Bolden was reputed to have a loud, rough, emotionally stirring style for ballads and blues. And it's safe to suppose Mumford was a very strong rhythm player. After Bolden stopped playing, Mumford continued as a musician for only a short time. In 1907, he opened a barbershop, and within a couple of years he was a full-time barber, playing only occasionally at family parties. Another early jazz guitarist was Bud Scott, also from New Orleans. Born in 1890, he studied music and played violin well enough to do symphony and theater jobs and worked with John Robichaux's well-known band that entertained on weekends in a park. Although Scott's name didn't usually appear, he played guitar on hundreds of recordings made with blues singers and early combos. Among the other leading early guitarists were the bluesmen Big Bill Broonzy, Huddie Ledbetter (nicknamed "Leadbelly"), Blind Willie McTell, Blind Lemon Jefferson, Robert Johnson, and Lonnie Johnson. Lonnie Johnson recorded with Eddie Lang, a well-known white, steel-string acoustic guitarist. All those players, except for Lang, were African-American and used their guitars as accompaniment for their singing. Up through the 1930s, these men played steel-string acoustic guitars, for there was no amplification at that time.

In the 1930s, the primary use of the acoustic guitar was for strumming the strings for the rhythm sections in big and middle-sized bands. Some of the main rhythm guitar players were Freddie Green with the Count Basie band, Fred Guy with Duke Ellington's orchestra, Allan Reuss with clarinetist Benny Goodman's band, and Connie Wainwright with pianist Earl Hines.

A few guitarists played solos in the 1930s. Among them were the versatile and popular Eddie Lang, who not only recorded with Lonnie Johnson but with violinist and bandleader Joe Venuti, star bandleader Paul Whiteman, and Bing Crosby, one of the most popular baritones in the history of jazz singing. Another guitarist, Teddy Bunn, played and recorded with the Spirits of Rhythm, a small group led by zany scat singer and tiple player Leo Watson. (A tiple is a transitional instrument between banjo and guitar.)In 1939, Teddy Bunn was the first jazz guitarist to record solo pieces for the adventurous little Blue Note record label.

The most influential guitarist in the 1930s was Django Reinhardt. A Belgian-born gypsy guitarist, who lived in France, he became a legend in such groups as the Hot Club of France Quintet, and in combos, sometime simply duos, with French jazz violinist Stephane Grappelli. Django was also known as a great soloist and composer. One of his most famous tunes, the whimsical, wistful "Nuages" is still played by musicians on all instruments. Young American musicians, and not just guitarists, hearing Django Reinhardt's recordings, became convinced they should commit their lives to jazz. Many guitarists learned to play by ear from his records.

Django Reinhardt (center, on guitar) and Stephane Grappelli (on violin) in the Hot Club of France Quintet

In 1938 and 1939, with the invention and marketing of the electric guitar, everything changed for the guitarists. Charlie Christian was the first major soloist on the amplified acoustic guitar—the electric guitar. It liberated guitarists, because it allowed them to become soloists with the power to be heard as well as saxophonists or trumpeters. The invention of the electric guitar coincided with a revolution in the jazz world. A handful of great innovators—primarily trumpeter Dizzy Gillespie, alto saxophonist Charlie "Bird" Parker, pianist Thelonious Monk, and drummer Kenny Clarke—developed a style called bebop. It was a sophisticated, more intense way of phrasing songs and of playing rhythms and harmonies, altering chords and playing substitute chords. Charlie Christian, playing long, flowing lines in the style of a horn player, on electric guitar, adopted some of the beboppers' innovations, particularly their rhythmic ones. He was a major soloist, as the style developed in the very early 1940s. Though essentially a swing-era guitarist, he was sufficiently gifted to keep up with the beboppers. In 1941, he was recorded live at Minton's. Those exciting recordings, showcasing Christian's energy and spirit, are still available today. Christian was a dominant force on all the tracks he recorded at Minton's, in especially brilliant interactions with drummer Clarke. Christian recorded with Benny Goodman and clarinetist Edmond Hall, too.

But in March 1942, Christian died. He was one of a number of jazz musicians who contracted tuberculosis, probably due to life on the road and substandard conditions, at a time when no cure was known for the disease. Thelonious Monk, who became one of the most individualistic pianists and composers in jazz, would always compare other guitarists to Charlie Christian and say there was never anyone better.

Several other great players followed Christian. All of them lived longer than he did and had their chances to establish recording careers and make themselves known to the general public. Among them were Barney Kessel and Herb Ellis. Both, at different times, played in a famous trio led by jazz pianist Oscar Peterson. Another prominent guitarist of the 1940s was Oscar Moore, who played in the studios in Los Angeles and then began playing and recording in 1937 with the Nat King Cole trio. Nat was struggling at that time in small clubs in Los

Angeles, before becoming famous in 1943. Remo Palmier was another distinguished player of this era.

Moore also led his own small groups on recordings and composed some pretty tunes, particularly "Beautiful Moons Ago," rerecorded in the 1990s by a new guitar star, John Pizzarelli, Jr. A Nat Cole aficionado, Pizzarelli was tipped off about Moore's song by veteran trumpeter Johnny "Tasty" Parker. Spurred by his avid curiosity—and perhaps also on the advice of his father, guitarist Bucky Pizzarelli—John Jr. sought out the song by Moore and included it in his repertoire.

All these players showed the influence of saxophonists and trumpeters—not only Charlie "Bird" Parker, but Lester Young, too. Lester played haunting solos with long lines and a languid tone on his tenor saxophone, becoming known first in Count Basie's original band in the late 1930s in Kansas City. Suddenly, the guitarists had the freedom to play similarly long lines.

In addition, the rhythm sections of bands became looser and didn't need the old-fashioned sound of a rhythm guitar anymore. Rhythm guitarists play four beats to the bar—ching ching ching ching—four chords. The important rhythmic emphasis, or rhythmic unit, was the quarter note in the swing era. But it changed to the the eighth note for a more intense feeling in the bebop era.

That is not to say that rhythm-guitar players became extinct. Count Basie's band employed Freddie Green for the rest of Basie's and then Green's life. Basie died in 1984, and Green lived only until 1987. Other bands, even a modern big band co-led by fluegelhornist Thad Jones and drummer Mel Lewis in the mid-1960s and formed to play Jones's compositions and arrangements, used a rhythm guitarist at first. But he didn't really fit in with the modern music and didn't stay with the group long. For the most part, guitarists developed as part of the mainstream and went in the direction of the bebop revolution.

After Charlie Christian died, Jimmy Raney assumed the position of a major developer in the late 1940s and early 1950s. Raney extended Christian's inclinations toward the bebop revolution. Raney applied to the guitar the harmonic innovations of Bird, Monk, and one of their heirs, Lennie Tristano, an important jazz player and teacher who was noted for his harmonies. Raney paid particular attention to European music and used techniques of European compositions in the construction of his own solos.

Raney sounded pure, with a musical, clean, undistorted sound well suited to his melodic and harmonic material. And he influenced his contemporaries, guitarists Tal Farlow, Johnny Smith, Billy Bauer, and Mundell Lowe, among many others in the early to mid-1950s. Farlow and Lowe, who became very well known, enjoyed long-lived careers for the rest of the century. Farlow went to live in virtual seclusion, however, and rarely performed in public. One of the greatest jazz recordings of all time, an intimate, relaxed album entitled *After Hours*, included Mundell Lowe as the guitarist along with singer Sarah Vaughan and bassist George Duvivier, on the Roulette label in July 1961.

"I felt proud of that album," Mundell Lowe would recall years later. "We recorded it in about three and a half hours, from six to nine-thirty, in a single evening." (That's a very short time in which to do any album.) "Teddy Reig [the producer] brought tables, food, and drinks to the studio on West 106th Street in Manhattan. Every song was recorded in one or two takes. Sassy's work was devoid of vocal tricks."[1] The instrumentalists, with their tight communion and exquisite taste, led her to sing with great control and to stress her jazz feeling and improvisational genius. There was none of the flamboyant vocalizing that characterized much of her other work. Critics praised the album. Producer Reig later told Mundell Lowe that it was the only album Vaughan ever made that earned any money.

In the late 1950s, individual stylists blossomed among the guitarists. All of them learned from what had preceded them, and they became giants of jazz guitar. The most important was Wes Montgomery, a native of Indianapolis, who had great soulfulness in his playing. He had tremendous technical facility with single note lines—lines composed of single notes, horn-like lines not made up of chords, or combinations of notes played at the same time. He mastered octaves and block chords, too, and had equal facility in all these areas. Because of his technique alone, his playing was high art. But most important, the music he played was so strong, so redolent of gravy and strong seasoning, with such an understanding of the blues, that he transcended the instrument. And he swung. He had everything going for him. Every guitarist—from his day to the present—studies Wes Montgomery's recordings.

One of these disciples was the exceptional Emily Remler, who lived a short, fast life in the 1980s. Before her death from a drug overdose while she was on tour in Australia, she made many recordings, naming one of them *East to Wes*. Although technically a modernist, because she was much younger than Wes, her performances and aesthetic goals belonged to his era artistically.

Other guitarists who emerged in this era of the flowering of great individualists were Kenny Burrell, Jim Hall, Grant Green, and Charlie Byrd. Burrell was important because he was not only a fine guitarist—and he still is—but he created a place for the guitar in the East Coast, hard bop combos in the 1950s that followed the bebop era. Burrell was one of the first guitarists to work often in the guitar, bass, and drums format.

Jim Hall, a great soloist and accompanist, was part of several important groups led by horn players in the late 1950s and early 1960s—such as saxophonist Jimmy Giuffre's trio, tenor saxophonist Sonny Rollins's quartet, and fluegelhornist and trumpeter Art Farmer's groups. Hall's playing was exemplary. He always chose the most expressive note and played it at precisely the right time.

Grant Green, who came to New York from St. Louis in the early 1960s, had a very strong blues influence. He was a great single note line player who recorded a great deal for the Blue Note label, worked with many organ groups, and played important solos on guitar with a clean, cutting, incisive sound.

Charlie Byrd became particularly well known for his performance on the first Stan Getz recording of Brazilian music. It was a very influential record, because it taught people about the lovely, romantic Brazilian music.

Brazilian music flowed in a parallel stream to jazz. Many American jazz musicians would discover and fall in love with Brazilian music. Some even predicted it was the music of the future and dabbled in trying to play it. But both Brazilian music and jazz have retained their identities and primarily reflect the cultures of their countries.

In the 1960s, great Brazilian guitarists and composers influenced Charlie Byrd. They included Antonio Carlos Jobim, Joao Gilberto, Luiz Bonfa, Oscar Castro-Neves, Laurindo Almeida, and Bola Sete. All of them eventually became known in the United States. (Milton Nascimento, an important Brazilian guitarist, singer and composer, would come along later, in the 1970s, popularized in the United States by tenor and soprano saxophonist Wayne Shorter.) They were playing *bossa nova*, which literally means "new bump"—as in a bump on the head—a bump signifying a development, not an injury, and so actually a "new idea" in its proper translation into English.

In 1962, Getz convinced his producer, Creed Taylor, to do an album of Brazilian songs, co-led by Charlie Byrd, for the Verve label. Byrd recruited the right musicians for the rhythmically demanding music. Taylor and Getz went to Washington, D.C., to record the album, *Jazz Samba*, in a hall with good acoustics. Creed chose that name instead of bossa nova so that Americans would understand right away what they were listening to. Though Byrd performed solos on the album, they were cut out of the final product in the interest of the length of songs. Getz won a Grammy award for the Best Solo, for a solo which he did on one of the upbeat songs. Since it was only Getz's solo that won the Grammy—and not the whole song and not the whole album—Byrd didn't share in the award. And though he was officially co-leader of the album, he received no royalties for it either. He got nowhere talking to Getz, so he sued and won some money as his share. The recording was enormously popular—bringing to the American public such tunes as "One Note Samba." Bossa nova became a new type of tune, a new form to play, and part of the everyday repertoires of American jazz musicians.

Another curiosity—essentially a sidelight—about the introduction of the bossa nova to the United States was the instant celebrity it brought to a young Brazilian housewife—Astrud Gilberto—for Getz's second bossa nova album. Married to guitarist Joao Gilberto, Astrud had never pursued a career as a singer. She had a very small, soft voice with a wavering intonation—that is, she didn't always sing in tune. But she sang the Brazilian songs at Stan Getz's request, before he did his recordings, because she was the only person on the project who could speak both English and Portuguese. Stan Getz liked the sensuous, casual quality of her voice and insisted she remain on the final recording of the song "The Girl from Ipanema." Her "promotion" from housewife to singer led to bitter arguments between Astrud and Joao, and by the time an album called *Getz/Gilberto*, which included her song, was finished in 1963, Joao and Astrud were divorced. She became a professional singer with a long-lived career and many fans in the United States. As late as the 1990s, this very attractive singer—or vocal personality—was a headline attraction at such leading jazz clubs in New York as Fat Tuesday.

In the late 1960s, the post-bop mainstream emerged, including such guitarists as Joe Pass, Pat Martino, George Benson, Gene Bertoncini, Attila Zoller, and Peter Leitch. Martino was a master of the long, eighth-note line, and he had a particularly fluid technique—more so than most other players. He could be fluid to the point of seeming too even and mechanical. George Benson had great technique, too; he was the most phenomenal technician of this group. But Benson, who was enormously gifted as a jazz player, went on to become a wealthy star in popular music. In the 1990s, he could command, it was said, $200,000 for performing twelve shows during one week at a Blue Note club in Japan. He developed a technique for singing in unison—for singing exactly the same note that he was playing on the guitar at the same moment; with the technique, he amplified himself. A few jazz players, particularly bassists, have sung in unison, too. But none of them became pop stars singing popular material the way Benson did, for such impressive material rewards.

Peter Leitch is included in the group that emerged in this era. He is particularly noted for his phrasing, articulation—in short his startling technique and taste. Without trying to produce fireworks, he plays fascinating, interesting music in his own quiet way. From the mid-1990s on, he performed regularly in duos in Walker's, a Manhattan club noted as a guitar room, with leading players such as saxophonist Gary Bartz. Leitch was one of the few guitarists ever to lead groups in Bradley's, a famed piano jazz room from 1969 to 1996 in New York. Kevin Eubanks and Russell Malone were among the few other guitarists to play there.

Joe Pass also had incredible technique. In his solo work, he combined his single note lines, chords, and walking bass lines. He was the first guitarist to perform solo jazz guitar on a grand scale, in one man concerts all over the world. He was to the guitar what Art Tatum was to the piano. Pass also recorded and performed to acclaim with singer Ella Fitzgerald, who was known as the First Lady of Song for nearly the entire second half of the twentieth century. Pass had a singing guitar.

Gene Bertoncini developed a very unusual, personal style of playing jazz on the nylon-string guitar, using the right-hand fingers in a classical style instead of a pick. Charlie Byrd played jazz on the nylon-string classical guitar, too, using the classical techique of playing with his fingers. And so did Washington guitarist Bill Harris in the 1950s and 1960s. But it was very unusual for jazz players to use nylon strings and pluck with their fingers.

Attila Zoller was so versatile that he won praise for his strong, straight-ahead mainstream playing as well as his free jazz recordings of abstract, atonal music. A Hungarian refugee, he toured in Europe and found himself particularly welcome in Germany, where his German last name gave employers the impression that he was of German background. For the same reason, he said, he never got bookings in France.[2]

Larry Coryell

He taught guitar at a school in Vermont, and he helped promote the careers of young guitarists. A brilliant musician and innovator, he worked with string manufacturers to develop a better string.

The next major development began in the 1970s and has lasted until the present time. Fusion—a fusion of jazz and pop music—emphasized an electric sound. Fusion was also characterized by an even eighth-note rhythmic feel, with a steadiness typical of rock music, instead of the looser and swinging triplet eighth note rhythmic feel of mainstream, acoustic jazz. Some of the major fusion players have been John McLaughlin, Larry Coryell, John Scofield, John Abercrombie, Pat Metheny, and Bill

Frisell. In a sense, Stanley Jordan, a phenomenal technician who plays in an individualistic way with both hands simultaneously, fits in here chronologically. It's his technique, above all, that distinguishes his performances. He taps the strings instead of strumming or plucking them and plays two independent musical lines at once.

Fusion players moved away from traditional jazz playing. John McLaughlin, who worked with trumpeter Miles Davis and drummer Tony Williams, was one of the first guitarists to use pop and rock influences in a jazz-related context. He is best known for his group, the Mahavishnu Orchestra. It played very loud, electric, experimental-sounding music in the 1970s.

As with all the other instrumentalists in jazz, and in pop and rock, too, guitarists reflected the social, cultural, and political changes and turmoil in the country. Competition arose between Russia and the United States. The Russians launched their *Sputnik* spacecraft in 1956. That prompted the Americans to pour money into education and improve the school system. Young people became better educated and better informed. As a result, some of them began to rock the boat and move toward changing society. Eventually their activism led to riots in the ghettos, protests against the war in Vietnam, the hippie movement, and counterculture lifestyles. The wild, original rock festival at Woodstock, New York, was among the more blatant examples of social protest.

Also worthy of examination is the entire post-World War II period. People who had lived through the war then worked hard to establish the status quo in the late 1940s. They wanted to acquire material wealth; they viewed their acquisitions as the true prizes of modern life—proof that they had survived and transcended a difficult past. To their children, however, the norms, standards, and goals of the postwar Eisenhower years—the 1950s—were meaningless platitudes that didn't reflect their personal feelings or aspirations. Slowly they began to erode the status quo by asserting their own interests. Then President John F. Kennedy caught the imagination of the younger generation. His assassination, which many people felt was never fully explained by official investigations, led to young people's dissatisfaction and distrust of government in general. Then Lyndon Johnson expanded American involvement in the Vietnam War, lying to the public about the necessity for the war and its goals. Young people became outraged. They protested, sometimes violently. The civil rights movement, with Johnson's staunch support, was beginning to succeed. But the ghettos were filled with angry souls, for whom progress was terribly slow.

All these elements had a strong effect on American culture. The new music—loud and very electric—was itself a type of elemental and primitive protest. The question arises: Was the popularity of loud, electric rock music the result of deeper thinking among young people? Or was it a scattershot, protest music—an explosively loud noise devised to block out thoughts about highly charged events, such as the assassinations, the controversial war, the frauds in high places—including the Nixon administration in the 1960s and 1970s, when the president lied about using criminal tactics to try defeat his political enemies?

In any case, people's horizons expanded—or, in some cases, seemingly exploded. Musicians—particularly rock and fusion jazz players—absorbed influences from everything happening in music, and from foreign, classical, and other non-jazz sources. These ranged from rocker Jerry Garcia to European composer Messaien to Indian sitar player Ravi Shankar as much as from John Coltrane and Charlie "Bird" Parker. Every type of music or earthly sound seemed to be a potential source of inspiration, or at least worthy of examination, especially for free jazz players, including the few guitarists among them. Eventually, a neo-classical movement developed. Budding jazz musicians returned to the style of Wes Montgomery and other players and giants of classic, pre-fusion jazz. Among the youngsters playing in an older style related to the pure tradition of jazz, with a warmer sound than the fusion musicians have, are Mark Whitfield, Peter Bernstein, and Russell Malone. They and many others are building successful careers in high profile clubs and concerts and on recordings.

CHAPTER TWO

The Blues Guitarists and Singers

It's impossible to say exactly where the blues ends and jazz begins, because the feeling of the blues has infused so much of jazz throughout its history. And jazz musicians still frequently play the blues—the pure blues, a folk music with its definite musical form. Usually it's a twelve-bar blues, though there are longer and shorter blues.

But it's definite that the guitar was one of the first instruments musicians used for playing the blues and then jazz. Jazz is a hybrid mixture of the blues and many other forms of music that evolved from the popular music styles in New Orleans in the first decade of the twentieth century.

Blues guitarists in the Southern states usually didn't play in groups. To a great extent, they were lone wolves whose lyrics expressed their personal stories and cares. They also sang songs that were part of the local legend and lore, and they adapted popular songs from one another, too.

Some blues guitarists were closer than others to playing in a jazz style. Not only did they improvise lines, or riffs—musical fills, ideas, and emphases to help them tell their stories—but some of them swung their rhythmic accompaniment. Among the Southern blues singers and guitarists most highly regarded by jazz musicians—and some of these bluesmen recorded with jazz groups—were Blind Lemon Jefferson, Lonnie Johnson, Blind Willie McTell, Big Bill Broonzy, Huddie "Leadbelly" Ledbetter, and Robert Johnson. All of them came from the south and made their way north, particularly to Chicago—the blues capital of the United States in the 1920s and 1930s. And they recorded in those years, too.

BLIND LEMON JEFFERSON

Lemon—which was his real name—was born in the tiny town of Couchman, Texas, and was the youngest child in the big family of Classie and Alec Jefferson. Though he was born blind, he seemed to handle his handicap very well, running and playing with other children.

Though he never went to school, by the time he was fourteen, he had taught himself to sing and accompany himself on the guitar, and he ventured off the farm to the nearby town of Wortham. In front of its grain and dry-goods store, he sang, played his guitar, and earned money from passersby to help pay for the family's food.

He became a popular entertainer in the area and played at picnics and parties on local farms.[1] It's possible that Lemon could have lived his whole life in the relative safety of his family's farm, but he decided to try his luck in Dallas, Texas—the big city. So at age twenty, in 1917, he told his parents good-bye.

He nearly starved to death singing on street corners, so he started wrestling in theaters for a living. The fact that he couldn't see his opponents made him a great novelty act. Luckily, he weighed about 250 pounds (113 kg),[2] so he never got hurt. As time went by, his fortunes as a street musician changed. He began working steadily in Dallas and at parties and dances in neighboring small towns.

One of his cousins, who lived in the area, noticed how rough Blind Lemon's lifestyle was. Blind Lemon played all night for men who were hustling liquor and women. Instead of complaining about his lot in life, he simply adapted to it, enjoying the liquor and women himself. In Dallas, he spent most of his time in the red light district, working in bars and brothels, sometimes with other singers who collected the money for him. He tried to hide his blindness by hugging the walls, playing until he had enough money to buy some liquor.

In 1922 or 1923, he married a woman named Roberta, and they had a son a few years later. Meanwhile he kept developing his musical talent. Eventually, he recorded a great variety of songs—field songs, hymns, city blues, country blues, and vaudeville songs. He learned every trick and style of blues guitar by ear. "The Texas men sang in a high, crying voice, with the biting tone of the guitar whining behind them. All the loneliness and poverty of the dry, empty fields of central Texas was in their singing. When Lemon left the streets and brothels of Dallas, his blues training was finished."[3]

Then he roamed in the region, from Alabama to Memphis and back to Texas. Famous by then, he attracted young, hopeful boys as assistants on the streets. Following him around, they tried to learn music from him by ear. He spent his money on liquor and women as quickly as he earned it. Naturally, he and his wife drifted apart. She went to stay with his parents at times, and neighbors in Couchman described her as a "quiet, mousy woman"[4] who had very little to say.

The Paramount Company learned about Blind Lemon and asked him to go to Chicago, where he made his first recordings in spring 1925, then more in 1926. His first record, "Long Lonesome Blues," and "Got the Blues" were hits for him and Paramount. His next release, "Black Horse Blues," was advertised in the African-American newspaper, the *Chicago Defender*.

An African-American man named Mayo Williams headed Paramount's race records division, which produced records to sell primarily in the African-American communities. He soon took charge of Blind Lemon's work. Williams was an important man in the field, but his relations with Blind Lemon were not ethical. For his recordings, Blind Lemon received a few dollars, a bottle of liquor, and a prostitute to dally with. Those were the only rewards that interested Blind Lemon. He may have only been drowning his sorrows and controlling the terrors of his blindness, but he was living the blues every moment of his life.

Another label, Okeh, recorded him in 1927, but Blind Lemon soon went back to Paramount. He ran out of songs he had learned in Texas and began singing the urban blues —songs about life's troubles, particularly sexual situations, in the big city. He worked sometimes with a pianist named George Perkins. In 1929, Blind Lemon was still popular enough to have Paramount release a record advertised in the *Chicago Defender* as a celebration of his birthday.

But the blues itself was declining in popularity because of the Depression. After the stock-market crash in 1929, people wanted to hear a more upbeat type of music to take their minds off their personal losses and miseries. Even so, Blind Lemon, thirty-three years old in 1930, still found jobs playing for parties, and he recorded often.

Once, after a recording session, he left a studio and headed for a party. It was a bitter cold and snowy night. He may already have been drunk. The next day, he was found dead, frozen in the snow, with his guitar lying beside him. His body was taken by train back to Texas and buried in a cemetery outside Wortham.

One of the blues songs he sang asked a "kind favor" of the world. Blind Lemon wanted his grave to be "kept clean."[5] But in his family's plot, only his mother and a sister had markers on their graves, which were almost lost in the weeds and grass under some trees. Blind Lemon's grave had nothing—a testimonial, if anything ever was, to the conditions that had inspired him to become a blues master.

LONNIE JOHNSON

Another gifted blues artist, particularly admired and remembered to this day for his guitar playing, was Lonnie Johnson. Born on February 8, in

Blues guitarist
Lonnie Johnson

either 1889 or 1894 in New Orleans,[6] he survived a disaster that could have crushed his spirit forever. Both his parents and all his brothers and sisters, except one brother, James, died in an influenza epidemic in 1915. Lonnie and James, also a musician, were playing professionally—James on guitar, violin, piano, and banjo—in their hometown. After so many deaths in the family, Lonnie, burdened with mourning, began traveling. He performed in a musical review that took him to England during World War I (1914–1918).

After the war, he returned to work in a St. Louis theater when band-leader Charlie Creath hired him. They worked on a Mississippi riverboat for a while, until they had a disagreement. Lonnie went to St. Louis, took a job in a steel foundry, got married, and won a blues contest in a theater. That victory led to his first recording for the Okeh label. Like Paramount, Okeh was a pioneer in the blues and race records field. Johnson was accompanied by a violin and piano, then was joined in his recording and personal appearances by his brother James on a variety of instruments. By 1927, Lonnie's recordings were selling very well. He had a striking sound on his metal-front guitar; he was inventive, fluid, and sweet.

Moving to New York with his wife, Mary, he recorded throughout the month of August 1927. His accompaniments for a new singer, Texas Alexander, on those recordings were notable for his "almost entirely melodic background, in a simple rhythmic imitation of [the singer's] deep voice." Lonnie also recorded his own song, "Mean Old Bed Bug Blues," released with "Roaming Rambler Blues," on the Okeh label in September. It was a big hit; at age thirty-eight, he was at the height of his success. Two months later, he recorded four sides with Louis Armstrong's classic Hot Five band. Louis inspired him to play striking solos and fiery, tasteful, rhythmic accompaniment. The next year, Lonnie recorded with Duke Ellington's band. Ellington, who was already successful and signed to another label, had to change his name on the recording to avoid contract difficulties; the group was billed as Lonnie Johnson and his Harlem Footwarmers.

In this period, Lonnie recorded his own personal, muted blues — songs about losing his job and his woman, who had taken his gifts and money — urban blues done in his soft, country style. To his blues singing, he brought the rich musical heritage and mixture of influences of his native New Orleans, and so his approach to the blues was quite sophisticated. He may have studied music — harmonies and chord progressions. In 1929, the first of his duet records with Eddie Lang, a great white guitarist of the period, was released. To circumvent racial prejudice that could interfere with the marketing of their work together, Lang used the name "Blind Willie Dunn." Their recordings were exciting, among the best guitar recordings ever made in the period, and they would stand the test of time.

In the early 1930s, he worked in Chicago clubs, such as the Three Deuces, with leading New Orleans drummer Baby Dodds and recorded for the Decca and Bluebird labels. In the 1940s, 1950s, and 1960s, his recordings became more pop-oriented. He began using the electric guitar—an amplified acoustic guitar—in the 1940s, and that instrument added to his modernized, pop feeling. By the late 1950s, a friend reported Lonnie was living in Cincinnati, possibly ill and without enough money. But with the later reissues of his recordings with Eddie Lang, he has exerted a strong influence on modern guitarists. He is thought to have died in Toronto, Canada, on June 16, 1970.[7]

BLIND WILLIE McTELL

In the excitement created by the success of the country blues singers and guitarists, several companies began sending field groups to the South to scout for talent. Then singers began arriving in the cities to look for recording opportunities. One of them was Blind Willie McTell, a Georgia singer and guitarist. McTell was brilliant and individualistic, but he was elusive. He slipped in and out of recording studios, making records for many companies under different names to avoid contract conflicts among Columbia, Okeh, Vocalian and Bluebird of the Victor company, probably his best sides, and Atlantic. In 1940, he recorded for John Lomax, the great folk and blues music aficionado, for the Library of Congress archives. But McTell's performances didn't please either John Lomax or his son Alan, and the material wasn't made available. In 1949, McTell, without talking about his past, simply walked into the Atlantic recording studios, auditioned, recorded, and then walked out and virtually disappeared.

He played a whining, biting, twelve-string guitar with savage style, and his singing was in the same vein. Even his lyrics had bite and wit. He sang one song about his recklessness and wildness after the death of his parents, and another about his lack of good looks though some sweet woman viewed him as an angel.

Three more eminent bluesmen were ***Big Bill Broonzy, Huddy Ledbetter***, and ***Robert Johnson***. Broonzy, born on June 26, 1893, in Mississippi and raised in Arkansas, had sixteen brothers and sisters—an enormous, impoverished family. As a child he made a crude violin out of a cigar box and entertained at parties and picnics. At age twenty-two, he married and worked his own farm. But he was cajoled into playing music again, when he was given a new violin and $50 for his efforts. His farm failed during a drought, and he took a job in a coal mine, went into the army for two years, and then, unable to stand racial bigotry in the South, moved to Chicago in search of a better life.

By the early 1930s, recording for the Bluebird label, he arrived at his own strong, strutting style, with a warm voice and an entertaining manner as a singer. In the 1930s and 1940s, he became a dominant force on the blues scene, holding copyrights to several hundred songs. He enjoyed success as a concert performer in the United States, England, and France, and recorded dozens of albums, singing urban and country blues as well as work songs. He had acquired a huge repertoire along the road of life.

Still very popular in the late 1950s, Big Bill became hoarse and was diagnosed with throat cancer; he couldn't sing or even talk anymore. Friends, including popular radio personality Studs Terkel, threw a benefit concert for him. In 1959, he died in an ambulance on the way to a hospital.

For a man who had lived such a rugged life, he had a bright outlook. In his 1955 book, *Big Bill Broonzy*, which he wrote and published with Cassell & Company Ltd. in London, he said he wanted to be remembered for the good times in his life. "Just write Big Bill was a well-known blues singer and player and has recorded 260 blues songs from 1925 up till 1952; he was a happy man when he was drunk and playing with women; he was liked by all the blues singers, some would get a little jealous sometimes but Bill would buy a bottle of whiskey and they all would start laughing and playing again, Big Bill would get drunk and slip off from the party and go home to sleep. . . ."

Huddy "Leadbelly" Ledbetter led a far more tumultuous life. Born in Louisiana around 1890, he was a guitar picker earning his living as an itinerant blues singer and player when he was sixteen. By that time, he may already have jumped bail in Shreveport, Louisiana. At age sixteen, he met Blind Lemon Jefferson in a saloon in Dallas and learned more about the blues. But Leadbelly disliked the city and was attracted

Big Bill Broonzy

to the rural blues, the work song, the ring shout, the field holler—a dramatic blend of early African-American music styles. And Leadbelly's unusual, mournful, even eerie sound had more in common with African than Western music.

He lived a wild life and was sentenced to the Louisiana Penitentiary for murder. While there, he sang and played his guitar and charmed the authorities with his music to such a degree that eventually they pardoned him. He is one of the best-known blues men in U.S. history, in part because of his distinctive artistry, and also because of his legendary, brawling lifestyle. In 1939, he played in a concert at Carnegie Hall, brought there by influential men connected with recording activities for the Library of Congress. In some versions of his life story, he is said to have died in a barroom brawl, but another story says he went to Chicago, where he was living with a wife, when he became ill from Lou Gehrig's disease and died.

Even less is known for sure about Robert Johnson, a "sullen and brooding" man[8] who had little contact with other blues men. He may have been raised in Mississippi; he was definitely poisoned by his girlfriend in San Antonio, Texas, in 1937. His fame rests upon recordings he made in 1936 and 1937 for the Vocalion label and several other less well-known labels under the auspices of the American Recording Corporation. Among his best-known recordings is "Hell Hound on My Trail."

The hell hound was the devil, who was omnipresent in his songs. He sang about the rocky road of his life. His images in his lyrics were imaginative, his voice was expressive, and his guitar playing intense and at times droning. In the blues world, he is a legend.

The primary connection between the blues men and the jazz players was the blues. The rhythm guitarists of the swing era, beginning in the 1920s and 1930s, played primarily in big bands and jazz combos. They heard recordings and live performances of some of the great blues artists and built their versatile careers on that foundation—the blues form and the feeling of the blues.

CHAPTER

THREE

Rhythm Players in the 1920s and 1930s

After the stock-market crash of 1929 and the Depression that followed, the popular music scene reflected the sense of devastation in the United States. Many people who had listened raptly to the blues stopped buying the records. They couldn't afford them, and they preferred the spiritual uplift of church music and swinging, big-band music. The big-band era was underway, starting slowly in the 1920s, gaining momentum in the 1930s, and peaking and declining in the 1940s. Many of the musicians in the bands were drafted in World War II (1939–1945). In their wake, small combos became popular. But while the big-band era flourished, many bands included guitarists in their rhythm sections. These guitarists almost never took solos; they strummed the rhythms.

FREDDIE GREEN

One of the best-known big-band guitarists was Freddie Green, an acoustic guitar player with the Count Basie band beginning in 1937. He stayed with that band until 1987, three years after Basie died. Basie's band continued playing under other leaders.

Born in Charleston, South Carolina, on March 31, 1911, Green played banjo at an early age, but a family friend urged him to switch to guitar and study music. According to one source, Green's parents died when he was twelve; after that he went to live in New York City with an aunt. He worked as an upholsterer by day and played the guitar at night.[1] Another source says Green didn't go to New York until 1930, but in any case, in 1936, he worked with drummer Kenny Clarke,[2] who would become a major innovator for the bebop revolution of the 1940s.

Green never moved in that direction but remained a powerful, reliable rhythm player with a light touch. He made only occasional forays into obligato accompaniment and very short solos on acoustic guitar. Other musicians respected his eminence as a rhythm player who strummed chords on each beat of the bar.

Green recorded with many groups throughout his career, but he's best-known for his work with Count Basie's band. In the mid-1930s, Basie began leading his own band in Kansas City. Clarinetist Benny Goodman discovered Basie's band on short-wave-radio broadcasts from the Reno Club. He told a friend, talent scout John Hammond, who rushed to Kansas City and signed Basie to recording and management contracts. The band recorded blues songs with singer Jimmy Rushing, toured the South, and made its way to New York City, where after a period of adjustment, the band became popular. The band needed a new guitarist to replace Claude "Fiddler" Williams, a rhythm guitarist and violinist who had begun playing guitar with Basie in 1936. (Before that, Williams had played in a well-known territory band called the Clouds of Joy led by saxophonist Andy Kirk. Williams had even played with Nat King Cole in Chicago before young Nat set out for Los Angeles.) Exactly why Williams left Basie isn't clear, but John Hammond heard

Freddie Green
(on guitar)

Freddie Green play in a Greenwich Village club and thought that, with his precise beat, Green would be ideal for Basie's blues-based band. He was auditioned and hired for what turned out to be a lifetime job. Soon after he took the job, he studied for a short time with Allan Reuss, a guitarist who played in Benny Goodman's band. According to several sources in the jazz world, Green was probably married twice and may have been between wives in 1938. That's when the great jazz singer Billie Holiday traveled with the Basie band. Freddie Green was definitely her boyfriend for a while on the road. Billie and Freddie were a perfect example of opposites attracting. Freddie was a steady, reliable man in the jazz world, while Billie lived a very wild life. It was said that Freddie, who could be a bit cranky and set in his ways, never got over Basie's death. But Freddie had played golf and maintained his health carefully despite all the rigors of life on the road. He died in Las Vegas, Nevada, on March 1, 1987.

ALLAN REUSS

Born on June 15, 1915, in New York City, Reuss, a white musician, studied with George Van Eps, who played guitar in Benny Goodman's band. In 1934 or 1935, Reuss replaced Van Eps in the Goodman band and stayed with it until 1938. He then branched out to play with other important swing-era band leaders—Paul Whiteman, whose band nurtured many jazz instrumentalists and singers; trombonist Jack Teagarden, famed for his work with Louis Armstrong as well as with his own groups; the bandleader-saxophonist Jimmy Dorsey; Ted Weems's band; and the NBC band in Chicago. These were illustrious names in the swing era.

In 1943, Reuss went back to Goodman, then on to trumpeter-bandleader Harry James in 1944. Reuss played often in studios for recordings, working with famous musicians—both whites and African-Americans. Known for his teaching abilities throughout his career and categorized as a swing-era rhythm guitarist—and one of the best who ever lived—Reuss also could play rhythmic chordal melodies and single-string solos on his acoustic guitar.

FRED GUY

Like many guitarists of his era, Fred Guy began his career playing the banjo. Born in a small town in Georgia on May 23, 1897, he migrated to New York and led his own band at a club called The Oriental. Then he moved on to play with Duke Ellington's band in 1925. He was still playing banjo at that time and didn't switch to guitar until 1934, probably because it was so much easier for him to make himself heard on banjo before acoustic guitars were amplified. After making the switch to guitar, he remained with Duke's band until 1949, playing in the rhythm section, never as a soloist. He kept the band oriented with his steady beat.

When he left Duke, Guy went to Chicago and managed a ballroom for about twenty years. Duke never hired another guitarist. At least one reason was that times had changed. By the late 1940s, bebop innovations had given rise to an era of individualistic guitarists who were no longer restricted to rhythm playing.

Other notable guitarists from the swing era included *Connie Wainwright*. He probably studied with Allan Reuss, definitely played with pianist Earl Hines's very popular band in the 1940s and then with the first bebop band led by singer Billy Eckstine. But Wainwright was never a bebopper, always a rhythm player.

New Orleans banjoist and guitarist *Danny Barker*, born on January 13, 1909, went to New York where he played with many important artists in the 1930s and 1940s, including Cab Calloway's band in 1940. He was one of the few people who could also say he had played with King Oliver, Jelly Roll Morton, Charlie Parker, and Dizzy Gillespie. In Cab's band, Danny became friendly with Dizzy and encouraged the young trumpeter to keep experimenting with harmonies.

Married to the blues singer Blue Lu Barker, Danny formed a group to accompany her, and he continued to freelance, playing in the early, traditional style. He even played with his uncle—well-known, New Orleans-born drummer Paul Barbarin. Danny again began concentrating on banjo, of which he was a master. Returning to New Orleans in 1965, he became an assistant curator of the New Orleans Jazz Museum and the grand marshal of the Onward Brass Band.

In 1991, after a long life in jazz, Danny was designated a jazz master by the National Endowment for the Humanities and included in the Jazz Hall of Fame. He "was one of the best rhythm-section guitarists in all of jazz. It was his jazz pulse—through the time zones of various jazz styles—that enabled him to be at home with swingers, boppers, and homeboys."[3]

When he returned home, devoted to the music and traditions of New Orleans, Danny organized the Fairview Baptist Church Marching Band. He gathered children to teach them his city's musical legend and lore, traditional feelings, and the songs themselves—old songs such as

"Over in the Glory Land," "When the Saints Go Marching In," and "Bye and Bye." Young Wynton Marsalis and his brother Branford, who would become jazz superstars in the 1980s and 1990s, played in Danny's band. And Danny performed often in all kinds of groups until his death at age eighty-five in March 1994. He was treated to a splendid Second Line funeral, a New Orleans tradition. His band had forty musicians or more along with six grand marshals and hundreds of people in the Second Line—the people who followed the funeral procession, playing a dirge, along the route to the cemetery. Then they picked up the tempo for the trip back home.

Eddie Durham, born in Texas in 1909, became known as a trombonist and arranger. But he also played guitar in many swing-era bands. While with Jimmy Lunceford, an important African-American bandleader of the era, Durham began to experiment with ways of amplifying his guitar. Electric guitars didn't exist at that time. "With an aluminum resonator attached to his instrument, he made the first recorded jazz solo on an 'amplified' guitar on a [1935] recording called 'Hittin' the Bottle' with the Lunceford band."[4] In 1937 in Oklahoma City, he met a young guitarist named Charlie Christian and showed him his electrically amplified guitar. It had a terrific impact on Christian and on modern jazz.

Durham's greatest achievement was amplifying his guitar. The invention changed the course of guitar history, of jazz, and eventually of modern popular music in every style. In 1938, Durham recorded with a group called the Kansas City Six, which featured tenor saxophonist Lester Young and included Durham's electrically amplified guitar solos.

Floyd Smith, born in St. Louis, Missouri, in 1917, was another swing-era guitar player who was introduced to the amplified guitar by Eddie Durham. In 1939, Smith made the hit record *Floyd's Guitar Blues*, playing with the Andy Kirk band. Their recording helped boost the fortunes of the amplified guitar.

Al Casey led the house band at the Down Beat club on West 52nd Street—Swing Street—and played and recorded there, too, with pianist Teddy Wilson and Billie Holiday. He was also well known for his work

Floyd Smith, here playing a Hawaiian steel guitar

with Fats Waller, the pianist and composer. Casey was an *Esquire* magazine Gold Star winner twice in the 1940s, and recorded with an *Esquire* All-Star band in 1943, including Coleman Hawkins on tenor saxophone, Cootie Williams on trumpet, Edmond Hall on clarinet, Art Tatum on piano, Oscar Pettiford on bass, and Big Sid Catlett on drums—a memorable, vital group in which Casey's fine rhythm-guitar playing stood out.

Casey said that indispensable qualities for a guitarist were to know about the music—the chords and the background—and to become immersed in the styles and characteristics of other people in a group. The longer Casey worked in a group, the easier it had always been for him to play well in that particular setting. He thought that Freddie Green had excelled with Basie's band because he and Basie had enjoyed such a long relationship. Green became adept at inventing voicings—adding notes to ordinary chords to jibe with the piano and the bass.[5]

CHAPTER FOUR
Swing-Era Soloists

As early as the 1920s, some guitarists refused to be bound by the limits of the rhythm sections. These guitarists became pioneers in a variety of ways, primarily for their single-note solos. One of the most important, versatile guitarists in this era was Eddie Lang, a true renaissance man of the guitar.

EDDIE LANG

Born in Philadelphia on October 25, in either 1902 or 1904, Salvatore Massaro changed his name to Eddie Lang in honor of a basketball player whom he admired. First, Eddie studied the violin and sight singing, and then he began to teach himself to play the guitar on an instrument his father built for him. It was probably his early training

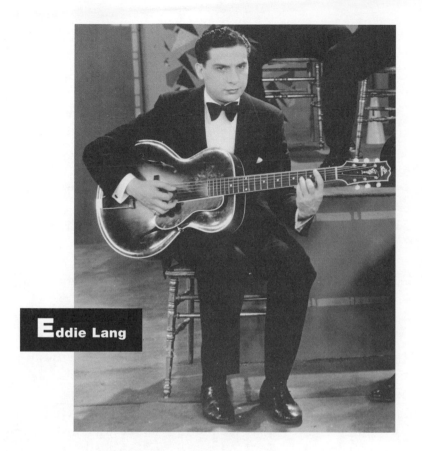

Eddie Lang

as a sight singer that intrigued him, taught him a great deal about the essence of music, and led him to explore the possibilities of playing single-note lines on the guitar.

In high school, Lang began a lifelong friendship with a violinist named Joe Venuti, a fun-loving, mischievous man and a swinging jazz player with a fine ear. Among his many attributes, Venuti could play double stops—two notes at once—perfectly in tune. Lang and Venuti often worked together.

In the early 1920s, Lang played banjo with several bands in Philadelphia and Atlantic City, and in 1924 he sat in as the guitarist with the Mound City Blue Blowers, a novelty group. They were a motley crew musically—"three noisy white amateurs from St. Louis—two soda jerks and an overweight ex-jockey."[1] One played banjo, another played a comb wrapped in tissue paper, and the third played a kazoo—a toy horn that vibrates with humming. Very loudly and very well, they imitated old-fashioned, African-American street corner bands—musicians who stood on street corners in such cities as New Orleans and tried to see who could play the loudest.

The Mound City Blue Blowers recorded *Blue Blues* and *Arkansas Blue* on the Brunswick label, which had excellent distribution. With Eddie Lang on guitar for *Arkansas Blue*, the recording became a great hit. Eddie's "uncommon sound . . . added harmonic flesh and rhythmic bones to the rather rickety sound of the little group."[2]

Another recording by Lang with the group, *Deep Second Street Blues*, showed that Eddie had a special feeling for the blues and could express himself with deep pathos in that Southern folk idiom. And as a rhythm player—maintaining an even four beats to the bar, in the way swing-era bands would do for a modern-sounding flow, Eddie often improvised with new chord positions, and inverted chords—inversions are the order in which the notes of a chord are arranged—and altered chords with raised (sharped) or lowered (flatted) notes. Not the least of his attributes was his lovely tone. He also was a master of vibrato. And he knew how to touch the strings so lightly that he could suggest overtones—notes an octave higher than the actual fret positions he was playing. These were among the many striking hallmarks of his mature work.

Bing Crosby, a young singer in Spokane, Washington, loved *Arkansas Blue* and tried to imitate aspects of it. This was his first contact with Eddie Lang. Bing and Lang would become musical colleagues and personal friends a few years later.

Lang played the Palace in New York with the group, toured England, then returned to the United States. In Atlantic City, Joe Venuti sat in with the Mound City Blue Blowers. Then in 1925, Lang left the group and free-lanced with many musicians, especially Venuti.

Lang and Venuti played together with several big bands, particularly Jean Goldkette's, and in that band, Eddie Lang's single-note playing was dazzling. Arrangers paid attention to the guitar's potential as an instrument that could take solos and began writing parts for it. Banjo players perked up their ears. Many switched to guitar. Beginning in 1926, Lang and Venuti recorded together very often. Some of Lang's best recordings were done with Venuti between 1927 and 1930. In 1927, Lang became a featured soloist with a group called Red Nichols and his Five Pennies. And Lang had calls to play with many top bands and also with blues singer Bessie Smith.

He paid particular attention to the blues players and loved Lonnie Johnson's work so much that he made sure he recorded with Johnson. Their exciting tracks are still available on CDs today. Lang was earning high fees for recordings and radio shows. He recorded with such jazz stars as trumpeter Louis Armstrong and trombonist Jack Teagarden.

In 1929, Paul Whiteman, a very popular bandleader, hired Joe Venuti and Eddie Lang as a team. Bing Crosby was singing with Whiteman in a vocal trio called The Rhythm Boys at that time. In 1930, after he discovered that he was a big hit at the Cocoanut Grove in Los Angeles, Bing left Whiteman to pursue a career as a romantic solo singer. Taking Lang along, Bing headed for a major success at the Paramount theater in New York. Eddie, with his perfect pitch and ability to memorize music quickly, worked steadily with Bing and played many other jobs on the side.

Another guitarist, Jack Bland, said that Lang had the best ear of any musician he had ever known. "He could go into another room and hit A and come back and play cards for fifteen minutes, and then tune his instrument perfectly. I've seen that happen."[3] Lang also appeared briefly in Bing's movie *The Big Broadcast of 1932*.

But Lang had been suffering with a chronically inflamed sore throat for more than a year in the early 1930s. He disliked and feared doctors and stubbornly refused to see one for a long time. Bing finally talked him into seeking treatment. "Many times afterward I wished I hadn't," Bing later wrote in his autobiography. "The doctor advised a tonsillectomy, and Eddie never came out from under the general anesthetic they gave him . . . [he] developed an embolism and died without regaining consciousness."[4]

OSCAR MOORE

Oscar Moore was born on Christmas Day 1916 in Austin, Texas, and moved to Phoenix, Arizona, in the early 1930s with his musical family, including his guitar-playing elder brother, Johnny. Oscar learned to play the guitar by listening to Johnny but quickly surpassed his brother as a player. Soon musicians passing through town learned about Oscar's immense talent.

In 1936, Oscar went to Los Angeles, where he was on the list of the first musicians to be called by MGM, among other studios. He played the guitar that Mickey Rooney mimed strumming in the movie *Girl Crazy*. In 1937, a struggling young pianist named Nat King Cole was asked to organize a small group to play at the Swanee Inn, a musicians' hangout, for a few weeks. Nat said sure, he could do that. The pay was $75 a week for the group. Nat recruited bassist Wesley Prince, who was leaving Lionel Hampton's band. Prince had a friend, Oscar, who played guitar with lyricism and imagination. Nat may have known Oscar anyway. All the young musicians on the scene in Los Angeles knew or had heard about one another. They traveled in the same circles and had a lively grapevine. Nat himself said, "The way we got together was the most natural thing in the world. When I was playing around town, I ran into Oscar Moore and then Wesley Prince. Seemed like a good idea to get a group together."[5] Nat discovered that Oscar was the guitarist with everything—great rhythmic and melodic feeling, improvisatory genius, soloing charisma, and sensitivity to the musicians with whom he played. Later on, in the 1940s, Oscar confided to a fan that he had idolized Eddie Lang and also the Belgian-born gypsy guitarist Django Reinhardt. Oscar and Nat had a special communion, Oscar with his ringing, lyrical guitar, and Nat with his imaginative pulsing piano, both of them brilliant soloists for the group. And each man in the trio communicated well with the others, emanating from one another's lines with special accents. So strong was their rhythmic feeling that they didn't even need a drummer. For six months, the group remained at the Swanee Inn and acquired its name—the King Cole Trio.

The trio struggled along for seven lean years. There was a change of bassists, but Oscar remained. Like Nat, Oscar was raised in the swing era but was so contemporary that he defied labels. Both heralded the more progressive jazz style that began emerging in 1940 in Harlem—bebop. And their harmonies and improvisations were new and surprising to audiences. Oscar played so clearly and articulately that he set a standard never really surpassed for quality and fluidity. His work never sounded outdated.

By 1943, the trio had found a manager who signed them to a new label, Capitol, and booked them into theaters. One of their first releases, "Vom Vim Veedle," made the charts in 1943. Then their record, *Straighten Up and Fly Right*, became a hit in 1944. Their weekly pay went from $225 at a little Los Angeles club to $1,000 at the Orpheum Theater in 1944.

Between 1944 and 1946, Oscar earned $1,500 a week, plus very big bonuses at Christmastime. Royalties for recordings went to Nat, the group leader. But he paid his sidemen the bonuses to reward them. After a while, according to Oscar's friends, Oscar wanted to join his brother Johnny's group, The Three Blazers. Each time Oscar mentioned quitting Nat's trio, Nat raised his salary.

But in 1946, Nat's new wife clashed with his sidemen. She treated them like servants, and she wielded a great deal of influence over Nat.

The tensions worsened. At the same time, Oscar had become so recognized by critics and the public that he had been invited to lead his own record, including tunes he had written such as "Up Tempo" and "Walkin' Home," sometimes available on the V.S.O.P. label in big record stores. Another of his tunes, "Beautiful Moons Ago," recorded with Nat's trio, was put out on a Savoy CD in 1989.

Oscar won the *Down Beat* magazine Readers Poll and the *Metronome* magazine poll for his guitar-playing every year from 1945 through 1948. He also won the *Esquire* magazine Silver Award in 1944 and 1945 and the *Esquire* magazine Gold Award in 1946 and 1947. He was an ideal colleague for Nat, who also won awards from the same magazines in the 1940s. At that time those awards were among the most prestigious in the jazz world.

In 1946, Oscar quit the trio and became the featured player in his brother's group. So Oscar realized a dream. But it was his tense relationship with Nat's wife that had pushed him to move on. He never again achieved the fame that he had enjoyed with Nat's trio. He sued Nat for more money, and he got it. He and Nat had little or no contact from that time on. The bassist in the group quit, and he sued Nat, too.

When Nat King Cole died in 1965, he had become a national hero. But his original sidemen lived in obscurity. Oscar walked into the mausoleum at Forest Lawn Cemetery in Los Angeles, where Nat's body was on view. "Oscar sat down in front of the crypt, looked at Nat, then shook hands with the Cole family members,"[6] and with Nat's valet, Sparky Tavares. "Sparky was especially struck by the way Oscar Moore looked quietly at Nat and didn't stop to speak with anyone."[7] Moore simply walked out.

After playing with his brother's group, Oscar had worked with Ray Charles, Floyd Dixon, and in groups with Carl Perkins and Joe Comfort—good jazz musicians. But none of them except Ray Charles ever became big stars. Oscar made a few records on small labels such as Swing Time and Aladdin, but his life was a struggle. By the end of the 1950s, he worked as a bricklayer. In 1965, he recorded an LP as a tribute to Nat. Oscar died on October 8, 1981, in Las Vegas.

TEDDY BUNN

Born in Freeport, Long Island, in 1909, Teddy Bunn, basically a swing-era player, was especially swinging, inventive, and technically proficient. He is best remembered for his work with a very popular group in the 1930s and 1940s—the Spirits of Rhythm—fronted by zany scat singer Leo Watson, who also played trombone, drums, and tiple. The group starred at the Onyx club on West 52nd Street—Swing Street—and made recordings dominated by Watson's scat singing.

Bunn, who was self-taught, worked in the 1920s with blues singers and the Washboard Serenaders. Then he replaced Freddie Guy in Duke Ellington's orchestra for a while and even recorded with Ellington. For his solo playing, Bunn used his right thumb instead of a pick.

In 1937, Bunn left the Spirits of Rhythm. That was the year Leo Watson recorded with Artie Shaw and went on the road with Gene Krupa's band. Bunn went on to play with a popular band led by John Kirby, but in 1939 he rejoined the Spirits of Rhythm. Watson had been fired from Krupa's band for slashing a window shade on a train, and then when a conductor protested, Watson put his hand through the window. His talent transcended that incident—and many more like them—for a while. Bunn's talent shone with the Spirits of Rhythm. But then the group broke up.

By the early 1940s, Bunn led his own group called the Waves of Rhythm and other small bands in California. It isn't certain whether he played with the following groups between 1937 and 1939, or after World War II ended. But he did freelance with well-known, traditional, early jazz musicians such as clarinetists Johnny Dodds, Jimmie Noone, and Mezz Mezzrow. In the early 1940s, Bunn began playing the amplified acoustic guitar—the electric guitar favored by jazz players. He worked with the old bandleader Edgar Hayes and visited Hawaii with Jack McVea, played with the leading rock-and-roll saxophonist and singer Louis Jordan, and with other rock-and-roll players in the 1950s. In his last years, he suffered from a long illness and died in a California hospital on July 20, 1978.

Tiny Grimes and *Eddie Condon* were among the other notable guitarists of this era. Tiny's death in New York City on March 4, 1989, brought an outpouring of affection for him from the jazz community. Musicians turned out in droves for his memorial service at St. Peter's Lutheran Church, the jazz ministry in New York City. He had been such a well-liked man and a respected musician.

Born in 1916 or 1917 in Newport News, Virginia, Tiny first played drums in his school band. He switched to the piano and began to dance professionally in Washington, D.C., when he was twenty years old. From there he moved to New York and changed instruments once again, teaching himself to play the four-string guitar. It was another transitional instrument between the banjo and the six-string guitar. When everyone else switched to the six-string electric guitar, under the influence of Charlie Christian, who popularized that instrument, Tiny switched to an electric four-string guitar. And from it, he wrested a great deal of beautiful music.

In 1940, he worked with a spirited, rhythmically superior, popular jazz group called The Cats and a Fiddle, which had a hit with "I Miss You So." Then in 1944 he moved to California where he met the master pianist Art Tatum in a jam session. Tatum liked Grimes's work so much that he invited Tiny to join his trio with bassist Slam Stewart. Over a three-year period, the trio made historic recordings that are available now on CDs.

Grimes returned to New York City in the mid-1940s and worked on 52nd Street with leading jazz musicians of the day. In 1944, he recorded with his own trio, and alto saxophonist Charlie "Bird" Parker as guest, for tunes called "Tiny's Tempo," "I'll Always Love You Just the Same," "Red Cross," and "Romance Without Finance Is a Nuisance." He worked with his own group, the Rocking Highlanders, which achieved some measure of popularity for a while.

Then Grimes moved around—to Cleveland, then Philadelphia, and returned to New York City in the 1960s, playing in Harlem and Green-

Tiny Grimes (right) with trumpeter Roy Eldridge

wich Village clubs. Rock and roll dominated the pop music world. Grimes never achieved financial stability. But he could swing hard, he had a bluesy feeling, and he could play in a fleet, single-note style that won fans in the United States and abroad, particularly in France. A versatile musician, he freelanced with many groups from swing to bebop in New York during the last years of his life.

Eddie Condon played a four-string guitar, too. He began on ukelele, switched to banjo, and then went on to the guitar. Born in Goodland,

Indiana, in 1905, and raised in a Chicago suburb, Condon played with dance bands and joined the Austin High School Gang, a well-known white group that epitomized early jazz in the Chicago style. After leading a band for a while, and recording with the Chicagoans, a group that he co-led with Red McKenzie, Condon moved to New York in 1928. He recorded there into the 1970s. The list of musicians who played with Condon reads like a Who's Who of swing-era and early jazz, including Red McKenzie and the Mound City Blue Blowers, Fats Waller, and Louis Armstrong. In New York City, Condon played at a club called Nick's, a landmark for Dixieland music in Greenwich Village.

He is especially remembered for his ribald sense of humor. When he opened his own club, Condon's, in the Village in the mid-1940s, musicians loved to gather there. He once said that he didn't like the way French critics wrote about jazz. After all, he didn't tell them how to jump on a grape. He also said about Stan Kenton's big, bebop band that it sounded as if Kenton had sent out a call for 300 musicians for a rehearsal and all of them had showed up. He wrote several books that are sometimes available in stores and in libraries with jazz sections: *We Called It Music: A Generation of Jazz*, *Eddie Condon's Treasury of Jazz*, and *Eddie Condon's Scrapbook of Jazz*.

His club eventually moved uptown. He insisted upon racially integrated bands in his club and on television programs as well as for a concert series he promoted at Town Hall and Carnegie Hall.

Condon toured England, Japan, Australia, and New Zealand with his own group in the 1950s and 1960s, and he appeared at jazz festivals in the United States. Never a virtuoso as a rhythm player, he was nevertheless an important group leader, responsible to a great degree for the revival of interest in his beloved "trad" jazz—New Orleans and hot, 1920s-style Chicago jazz.

CHAPTER FIVE

Django Reinhardt, the Legendary Gypsy Guitarist of France

The singing, romantic sound of Django Reinhardt's music on an acoustic, classical, Spanish-style, French-made guitar reached the United States on recordings in the 1930s. His long, flowing and floating, single-line melodies, played one note at a time thrilled audiences, and he especially influenced the way other jazz guitarists played. More than any other guitarist, Django established the guitar as an instrument for soloing and unshackled it from the rhythm section.

Django, whose real name was Jean Baptiste Reinhardt, was born into a gypsy family in Liverchies, Belgium, on January 23, 1910. The family roamed through Belgium and France in a gypsy caravan; Django's father was an entertainer in a traveling show. Django began playing violin, then guitar and, as a young man, worked in the streets of Montmartre, famed as the artists' section of Paris.

His wife was a candle maker in their caravan, which camped outside of Paris. In 1928, some candles caught fire, and Django was badly burned. The third and fourth fingers of his left hand were so severely hurt that he could barely use them to play. He may have been able to play some simple chords with those crippled fingers on the first three strings of a guitar, but that was all. The accident didn't stop Django. He learned how to play with a very individualistic technique. It was all the more miraculous because he created his very fleet, lighter-than-air, single-string lines entirely with the first two fingers of his left hand.

After convalescing, he went back to the streets and cafés in Paris, working in the early 1930s in a duo with singer Jean Sablon. In 1934 he was recruited by Charles Delaunay, an eminent critic and entrepreneur for jazz in France, to play with a great jazz violinist, Stephane Grappelli. They had two other guitarists and a bassist in their group called the Quintet of the Hot Club of France. It toured in Europe and recorded a great deal. When the records reached the United States, Reinhardt became a celebrity.

American musicians visiting Europe made a point of playing and recording with him. Among the most important were "king of the tenor saxophone" Coleman Hawkins, alto saxophonist Benny Carter who traveled in England for many years, trumpeter Bill Coleman, trombonist Dickie Wells, and cornetist Rex Stewart of the Duke Ellington band. But most of all, Django would always be associated in the minds of his fans with Stephane Grappelli.

During World War II, Grappelli went to live and work in England. One of his jobs there was with pianist George Shearing, who would later become a star in the United States. The classy hotel where they played together in London was bombed, and they had to move on to other jobs. Most of the American jazz musicians went home to wait out the war. Django remained in France—a dangerous place for gypsies at that time—and toured Europe in his caravan. He led a band and played with a new quintet in which a clarinetist replaced Grappelli.

Django Reinhardt (left) with Duke Ellington

In 1946, Django visited the United States to tour with Duke Ellington's orchestra. Around this time, Django switched to an amplified guitar, though he always preferred his acoustic, French-made Maccaferri. Django's American adventure was full of difficulties. He had always been an unreliable character about time and even dates, showing up for some performances and not for others. Grappelli, with whom Django would work again after the war, would one day reminisce about the anxieties and tensions of working with Django. The mercurial guitarist once failed to show up for a command performance for French government officials, and Grappelli set out to find him. He was taking his leisure in a café, drinking with friends. Grappelli would say that he sometimes wished he could work with a more reliable person even if he might happen to be less of a genius.

Definitely, Django was a genius. His understanding of harmonies and his beautiful technique and sound made him a fine accompanist. As a soloist and improviser, he was mesmerizing. Though he couldn't read music, he composed lovely songs, of which his most famous is the moody, dreamy "Nuages," which means "clouds." Its sound can evoke the vision of clouds, even if a listener has no idea of the name of the song. A variety of jazz musicians on all instuments plays it to this day. Even John Pizzarelli, Jr., born eight years after Django died in 1953, recorded it in the 1990s.

The dapper, mustachioed Django, who never took care of his health, died young of a stroke. The legend is that he died after whiling away an afternoon fishing from the banks of the Seine River.

His brother, Joseph, a professional guitarist, who lived to be seventy, died in Paris, and was buried next to Django in Samois, France. Django's two sons—Henri "Lousson," by Django's first wife in 1929, and Babik, by his second wife in 1944—played guitar, too. Babik, an accomplished guitarist, established a professional career and played with his father. Then, for a while, Babik gave up playing, disheartened by the constant comparisons with Django. But in the 1980s he resumed playing professionally and enjoyed some success.

Several books and documentaries have been written and made about Django's life and legacy. One of the best-known books is *Django Reinhardt*, by Charles Delaunay, who knew Django personally from the Hot Club quintet days.

SIX

The Amplified Acoustic Guitar and Charlie Christian, and the Electric Solid-Body Guitar and Les Paul

In 1940, Charlie Christian was playing with Benny Goodman's band and jamming at night at Minton's Playhouse in Harlem, where a group of young revolutionaries was developing bebop. They were experimenting with substitute and alternate chords and new harmonies, and they were changing the phrasing and complicating the rhythms of jazz. Charlie Christian never explored the bebop innovations deeply. But he helped develop the foundation for modern jazz guitar on the electric guitar—the amplified acoustic guitar. He played long, single-note lines in the manner of horn players. And his understanding of harmonics and phrasing and rhythm allowed him to complement the beboppers. The carrying power of the electric guitar freed him to elevate the guitar to a soloist's instrument. And Charlie had a driving style and blues-influenced sound

Benny Goodman (seated) surrounded by his band, including Charlie Christian (behind Goodman with guitar)

that fit in well with bebop and contrasted sharply with the romantic sound and whimsy of Django Reinhardt. Most jazz writers came to believe that Charlie heard records by Django in the 1930s and fell under the gypsy's influence. But writer and musician Bill Simon, a close friend of people who knew Charlie in the days when he was playing with Goodman and the beboppers, doubted that Charlie was influenced by any one person in particular. He came from blues and country music territory—

Dallas, Texas, his birthplace in July 29, 1916, and Oklahoma City, where he grew up in a musical family in a very poor neighborhood. The guitar dominated the region's music. Charlie definitely heard the whining sound of the blues guitarists. And he undoubtedly retained a portion of their earthiness and crying emotionalism for his conception of jazz. He also heard music in a church across the street from his house. And he loved the music of such great jazz horn players as Lester Young on tenor saxophone. So Charlie was steeped in the fine music of the African-American culture.

In 1937, his path crossed Eddie Durham's when Durham passed through Oklahoma City, playing his newly amplified guitar. Christian began playing an electric guitar, too. Pianist-arranger Mary Lou Williams, touring the area with the Andy Kirk band, heard Charlie in Oklahoma City. She tipped off the hard-working jazz and blues talent scout, John Hammond. On his way to California to hear his brother-in-law, clarinetist Benny Goodman, record for Columbia records in 1939, Hammond made a side trip to Oklahoma City to hear Christian play.

Bill Simon told the amusing story of Hammond's side trip. Having notified Christian of his impending visit, Hammond got off a plane in Oklahoma City after a difficult flight. Hammond said he was "beat and bedraggled." And "To the 'horror' of his fellow passengers, an old wreck of a car drove up to the airport, jam-packed with six young Negroes." One of them was Charlie Christian, who introduced Hammond to the others, all players in his band. Hammond auditioned Charlie in the Ritz Cafe, where Charlie and his band worked several nights a week for $2.50 a person. Hammond thought the band was "simply horrible," he told Bill Simon, but Charlie could play so well that he was almost unbelievable.[1]

The next day, Hammond flew to Los Angeles and had a very hard time convincing Goodman to hire Charlie. But Hammond worked out a way to use him without ruining Goodman's budget. The band could obtain a guest fee from a Camel Caravan show Goodman was working for. Hammond sent for Christian, who arrived during a recording session with Goodman and several fine, professional musicians. Christian made a shocking entrance, because of the way he was dressed. He had no city sophistication of any kind. "Suddenly, in walks this vision, resplendent in a ten-gallon hat, pointed yellow shoes, a bright green suit over a purple shirt and, for the final elegant touch—a string bow tie. One man in the band, who happened to be color-blind, noticed that this character also toted a guitar and amplifier," wrote Simon.[2]

Benny Goodman refused to let Charlie join the session. After the date ended, he played one chorus of "Tea for Two" without an amplifier for Goodman, who ran out to a dinner appointment. But two men in the band felt bad for Charlie, who didn't seem to understand what was going on. Later that night, the musicians sneaked Charlie and his equipment onto the bandstand through the kitchen of a club where the Goodman band was playing. When Goodman saw Christian on the bandstand, it was too late. Christian was there for the performance. Goodman started the band playing the song "Rose Room," and the band played it "for forty-eight minutes!" Bill Simon wrote.[3]

"Apparently Charlie just kept feeding Benny riffs and rhythms and changes for chorus after chorus. That was Benny's first flight on an electronically amplified cloud." A few days later, when Benny set up his first sextet recording session, Charlie was in on it for "Flying Home." And Charlie was simply in. From a few dollars a week in Oklahoma, his salary suddenly jumped to $150 a week as a member of Goodman's organization. Goodman didn't really like an amplified guitar with his big band and kept Charlie restricted to the smaller groups much of the time. But Charlie had suddenly gone from "the backshack to the Big Time in one giant step," wrote Simon.[4]

Simon learned that Charlie had two overriding passions—music and women. He started to overdo it. He didn't obey the warning signs that he was becoming ill. Goodman sent him to his own doctor in Chicago, who saw scars from an old bout of tuberculosis and told Charlie to get enough rest and take care of himself. But Charlie was having too much fun.

When the Goodman band played at the Pennsylvania Hotel in New York in 1940, Charlie would finish his work for the night and jump into a taxi, his shirt still wet with perspiration, to jam at Minton's in Harlem. Teddy Hill, the manager of Minton's, and all the musicians there loved Charlie. "Minton's stayed open until four, which gave him about two and a half hours to wail all of the high-band jimmies out of his soul," wrote Simon. And on Monday nights, when the Goodman band didn't work, and most musicians were off, too, Charlie went to Minton's and played all night long. "Guitarists came to listen to him, not to cut him. That would have been impossible, and everyone knew it."[5]

Jerry Newman, a young jazz fan and amateur recording engineer who frequented Minton's, recorded the music on his own equipment, then raced to Columbia University's radio station and broadcast it. "[Jerry] recalls that Charlie most of the time would electrify the crowd with his riffing and his long-lined solos and his powerful drive, but that sometimes the stand would become jammed with battling no-talents, and Charlie would simply sit there and strum chords."[6]

Teddy Hill was so impressed that he bought Charlie an amplifier for $155, an expensive amplifier in those days. Then Charlie didn't have to bring his own heavy box to Minton's every night. Charlie, who smoked, put his lighted cigarettes on the amp, forgot about them, and created plenty of burn marks. Well-known musicians of the era used to go to Minton's to hear Charlie play—among them singer Lena Horne, pianist and composer Fats Waller, who wrote the song "Ain't Misbe-havin'," and the bebop creators Dizzy Gillespie and Charlie "Bird" Parker.

"Everybody loved Charlie [Christian]. The chicks mothered him, and the musicians kidded him good-naturedly . . . Teddy would tease him with, 'We're going to bring that Django over here, and he'll blow you right off that stand.' Charlie would break into a big grin and answer with a couple of slippery, typical Django phrases on his box."[7]

The men in the house band, pianist Thelonious Monk and drummer Kenny Clarke, loved Charlie Christian's playing, and so did Dizzy. Charlie loved them, too, and he even put up with the band's trumpeter, Joe Guy, who led the group but didn't play the best trumpet in the world. Guy said that if he was playing with Benny Goodman at the Pennsylvania Hotel, everyone would think he was great, too. But he sounded a lot better when Charlie was accompanying him.

Through the end of 1940 into the spring of 1941, Charlie played his heart out and romanced the girls who waited for him to play his last note. But then he became really sick, and he was sent to Seaview, a sanitarium on Staten Island. Count Basie asked his own doctor to take care of Charlie. Teddy Hill visited him once a week, too, and brought food from a woman who owned a restaurant popular with musicians. She baked a chicken without spices and a chocolate layer cake especially for Charlie free of charge. Hammond arranged for Charlie to have his guitar at the hospital.

Charlie was actually getting better. But something went wrong. Later on there were stories about some musicians who used to go the hospital and sneak Charlie out for parties with "combustible tea"—marijuana—[8] Simon wrote, as well as women and drinks. One cold night, Charlie had too much of the partying. Basie's doctor found out about it and put an end to it. But it was too late. Charlie had pneumonia. He died in March 1942. His legacy on recordings can thrill listeners. Jimmy Raney, a guitarist who didn't get to New York until 1944, would recall how he had been a teenager when he first heard Charlie's momentous recording of "Solo Flight" with the Goodman band. "Raney . . . believes that Charlie still stands on top of the heap, even when judged by the more modern standards. It was his sense of time, and of harmony—his way of outlining his chords without actually running them. The same observation has been made of Parker's playing on the alto sax," wrote Simon. Of all the recordings that Charlie made, none is a better example of his exciting guitar work than the recordings made by Jerry Newman at Minton's, and they are available in music stores. The Goodman sextet and septet recordings are the other most valuable Christian recordings. The great guitarists that followed in his footsteps and took his innovations farther along—Jimmy Raney, Barney Kessel, Tal Farlow, and Sal Salvador among them—were flattered when they were likened to Charlie Christian by the critics.

Les Paul, born in Waukesha, Wisconsin, on June 9, 1916, went to Chicago as a teenager and began jamming all over the South Side in the 1930s. Les made a point of going to that African-American neighborhood to jam with musicians because "they had it all together," he said.[9] He became close friends and hanging-out buddies with pianist Nat Cole, who was then a teenager. By 1938, Les went to New York City to play with Fred Waring's band. Leading his own group within that band, he was playing an electric guitar.

During the 1940s, Les was recognized as an outstanding guitarist and won many jazz polls. His style was influenced by Django, whom Les heard on recordings.

On July 2, 1944, Les was called for at the last moment to replace guitarist Oscar Moore at the first Jazz at the Philharmonic concert in Los Angeles, organized by jazz impresario Norman Granz. Les's colleagues in that concert included trombonist J. J. Johnson, tenor saxophonist Illinois Jacquet, and pianist Nat Cole. Because Les had to go AWOL from the army to play in that concert, he used the name Paul Leslie. The pseudonym was later discarded, and his real name appears on recordings now available.

Recalling that concert, for which he played such fiery music, Les said, "The first number we beat off. I threw my amp under the piano,

Husband and wife Les Paul and Mary Ford

and we took off. Nat and I had been playing together so much for so long. I had jammed every place he ever played. And we tore it apart. Nat and I chased each other; he played a run. I played a run. The pitch got so high, people were standing in their seats, screaming! Everyone was wearing a hat. And everyone threw a hat into the air, in the audience, everyplace. It was so exciting to see that. The concert made Norman Granz's career."[10]

Les's gifts as a guitarist have sometimes taken a backseat to his other remarkable accomplishments. First of all, he designed many solid-body electric guitars that bear his name, all made by the Gibson company. And as early as the 1930s, he began to experiment with developing multitrack recordings. Eventually he perfected and used the technique for his hit recordings with his wife, singer Mary Ford, in the 1950s.

When rock and roll swept the United States and then the world in the 1960s, Paul's solid-body electric guitar became more successful and famous than ever. In the 1980s and 1990s, despite his pain from arthritis, he was still performing in New York City jazz clubs—first Fat Tuesday, then the Iridium. He has won several Grammys from the National Academy of Recording Arts & Sciences for his contributions to the recording industry.

THE JAZZ GUITAR TREE

The development of the guitar's role in jazz was pushed along by leaps and bounds by the 1938 invention of the electric guitar, which is actually the amplified, hollow-body acoustic guitar, and then by the solid-body electric guitar. The solid-body electric guitar has been used primarily by rock-and-roll players. But jazz fusion players—musicians playing a blend, or fusion, of jazz and rock music beginning in the late 1960s—can use both the solid-body guitar and the hollow-body amplified acoustic guitar.

EARLY RHYTHM GUITARISTS IN JAZZ GROUPS

In the first decade of the twentieth century, **Brock Mumford** played rhythm guitar, and so did **Bud Scott**, in popular, early jazz groups in New Orleans. Mumford never recorded. Scott's work is docu-

mented on records, although his name rarely appeared on them.

BLUES GUITARISTS AND SINGERS

At the same time, U.S. blues guitarists and singers in the South and Southwest became popular entertainers. Usually they were solo performers, specializing in music from the rural areas where they were born and raised. Some of them migrated to big Southern cities and eventually, in the late 1910s and the 1920s, to Chicago—the blues capital of America at that time.

The most famous blues men included **Big Bill Broonzy, Huddy Ledbetter (nicknamed Leadbelly), Blind Willie McTell, Blind Lemon Jefferson, Robert Johnson,** and **Lonnie Johnson**.

All of them, with the exception of Robert Johnson, migrated north to Chicago to boost their careers and record. Big Bill Broonzy even visited England, where early blues and jazz stars were very popular. A biography was written about him.

Lonnie Johnson, who was born and raised in New Orleans, had the

Lonnie Johnson

keting of the recordings. Both Johnson and Lang, though rhythm guitarists, began playing solos with single-note lines on their acoustic guitars and hinted at the direction the guitarists would take in jazz.

SWING-ERA RHYTHM GUITARISTS

Blues guitarists and early rhythm and swing era guitarists had the blues in common. All of them played the blues, a folk music with a particular form, and usually a twelve-bar blues, though occasionally longer and shorter blues, too. And the feeling of the blues informed the work of the swing-era jazz guitarists even when they were playing other material.

The most important rhythm guitar players strummed the chords and didn't usually play solos in the swing era of the 1930s. They included **Freddie Green** with the Count Basie band, **Allan Reuss** with Benny Goodman's band, **Connie Wainwright** with Earl Hines's band, and **Teddy Bunn** with many groups, particularly the Spirits of Rhythm led by zany scat singer Leo Watson.

benefit of the rich, mixed cultural and musical heritage of that city, and he may have studied music. His material and rhythm guitar style were sufficiently sophisticated to attract the attention of swing-era guitarist **Eddie Lang**.

They recorded together. Lang used the name **Blind Willie Dunn**, to hide his identity. Lang was a white man, and Lonnie Johnson an African-American, at a time when segregation and prejudice made it difficult for musicians of different races to work together. By using a name that could pass for an African-American blues man's name, Lang got past the prejudice that would have hampered the mar-

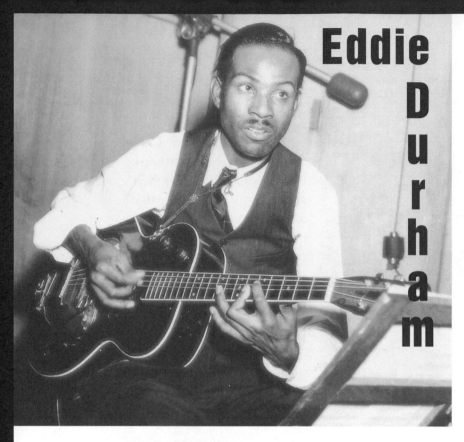

Eddie Durham

and with the legendary singer Bing Crosby. Lang, unfortunately, died of complications from a tonsillectomy in the early 1930s.

ELECTRIC GUITARISTS IN THE EARLY 1940S

Eddie Durham, a multi-instrumentalist, began playing his own invention, an amplified acoustic guitar, in the late 1930s. Passing through Oklahoma City, he showed off his invention to a young player, **Charlie Christian**, who immediately began playing one, too. The instrument suddenly allowed a guitarist to make himself heard in any group.

The invention of the electric guitar coincided with a revolution in the jazz world. A group of youngsters was inventing bebop—a sophisticated, intense way of phrasing songs and of playing rhythms and harmonies, altering chords and playing substitute chords. Charlie Christian began playing long, flowing lines, just as a horn player does, and adopted some of the bebopper's innovations. He was essentially a swing-era guitarist, but he was gifted enough to keep up with the beboppers.

In 1940 and 1941, Charlie made legendary recordings with Benny Good-

SOLO GUITARISTS IN THE SWING ERA

The most important of them all was **Django Reinhardt**, a Belgian-born gypsy guitarist and composer who lived primarily in France. When his romantic, whimsical solos and accompaniment on recordings made their way to the United States, American guitarists learned to copy Django by ear and became convinced they should devote their lives to jazz.

Few other guitarists were known as soloists at this time. Among them was Eddie Lang, an enormously admired musician. He played with jazz violinist **Joe Venuti**, with Paul Whiteman's famous swing-era band,

man's orchestra and with the young bebop-pers in the house band at Minton's Play-house in Harlem. Probably no more excit-ing music on guitar has ever been heard, and it has influenced guitarists for the rest of the century. In March 1942, Charlie Christian died of pneumonia after falling ill with tuberculosis.

ELECTRIC GUITARISTS IN THE LATE 1930S AND EARLY 1940S

Immediately following Christian came several players who learned from him and developed his ideas, playing long lines as the horn players and pianists did. These guitarists estab-lished the guitar as a soloist's instrument. Among them were **Barney Kessel** and **Herb Ellis**, both of whom would play with the famed trio of pianist Oscar Peter-son; **Oscar Moore** who played with Nat King Cole's group from 1937 to 1946; and **Remo Palmier**. Because of the invention of the electric guitar and the musical rev-olution called bebop, rhythm sec-tions in bands became looser and didn't need the steady four beats to the bar played by the rhythm gui-tarists. And the role of the guitar in jazz changed drastically from a background and accompanying instrument to a voice that could keep up with the front-line soloists.

Beginning in the late 1940s and continuing into the 1950s, one of the most important direct heirs of Charlie Christian was **Jimmy Raney**. He applied the harmonic innovations of the beboppers to the guitar. Raney also employed European music influences in the construction of his solos. Like Christian and Django, Raney influ-enced some of his excellent contempo-raries—**Tal Farlow**, **Johnny Smith**, **Billy Bauer**, and **Mundell Lowe**, among oth-ers. They played as leaders and accom-panists on classic recordings. Raney had a cool sound, compared with the pyrotechnics of the beboppers.

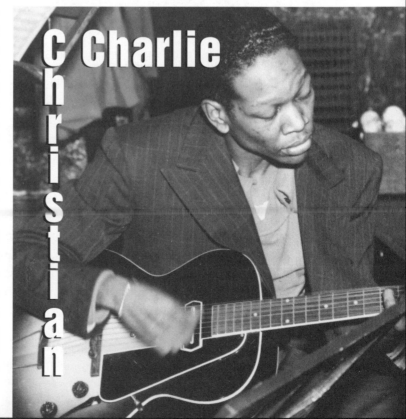

C Charlie Christian

Herb Ellis

Every jazz guitarist to this day studies Wes, and Christian and Django, too.

Among Wes's accomplished contemporaries, who were usually overshadowed by him at that time, were **Kenny Burrell, Jim Hall, Grant Green**, and **Charlie Byrd**. Burrell was particularly important for creating a prominent place for the guitar in small combos on the East Coast in the post-bebop or hard-bop era.

Jim Hall emerged as a great soloist and accompanist in this period. Grant Green had a strong blues influence and was exciting and highly praised as a player in two different worlds — jazz and rhythm and blues.

STYLISTS OF THE 1950S

Great stylists bloomed in this period. All of them built their styles on the innovators and developers of the two previous decades. The greatest of these stylists was **Wes Montgomery**, who had a wealth of soulfulness and a profound understanding of the blues, as well as tremendous technical facility with single-note lines. They were lines composed of single notes, horn-like lines not made up of chords or combinations of notes played at the same time. And he mastered octaves and block chords, too. These attributes, plus his ability to swing, meant that Wes had everything going for him.

AN INNOVATION OF THE EARLY 1960S

At that time, **Charlie Byrd**, already a noted stylist on the guitar, and a musician with a restlessly inquiring mind, brought the beautiful Brazilian music of the bossa nova — a combination of samba rhythms and jazz — to the attention of North Americans. With saxophonist Stan Getz, he co-led *Jazz Samba*, the very popular album of bossa nova in 1962.

THE POST-BEBOP MAIN-STREAM OF THE LATE 1960S

Joe Pass, Pat Martino, Gene Bertoncini, Attila Zoller, and **Peter Leitch** are included in this category of important stylists, virtuosos, and exploratory musicians. Of all of them, Joe Pass was famed for his great technique. He played solo concerts around the world, and he combined great single-note lines, chords, and walking bass lines in his appearances with his singing guitar.

Peter Leitch

A STAR OF OF THE LATE 1960S AND 1970S

George Benson, who became a popular figure in the jazz world in the 1960s, went on to take advantage of the growing popularity of electronics. Combining his jazz and rhythm and blues background with the values of popular music, he became a superstar as a singing guitarist in pop music in the mid-1970s. He also mastered the technique of playing in unison—that is, he played the exact note he was singing, thereby amplifying himself. Fans loved his sound and bought millions of copies of his recording of "Breezin'."

FUSION IN THE 1970S AND 1980S

Electronics took another giant step forward in American popular music beginning in 1969, when Miles Davis, the famed acoustic jazz trumpeter, went in search of a completely electronic sound. He used guitarist **John McLaughlin** on two important albums, *In a Silent Way* and *Bitches Brew*.

Many major fusion groups in the 1970s were founded by

musicians who had played on Miles's first electronic albums. Extremely important was John McLaughlin's group, Mahavishnu, which was very popular in the 1970s.

John McLaughlin

Other notable fusion guitarists were **Larry Coryell, John Scofield, John Abercrombie, Pat Metheny, Bill Frisell,** and **Robben Ford**, a founder of the group Yellowjackets, in the 1970s and 1980s.

The sheer loudness of their music attracted young listeners. They were becoming bored with acoustic jazz, and they wanted music that reflected the tumultuous times they were living in. The country was going through the civil rights movement, the war in Vietnam, the hippie movement, the political assassinations, and the revelations of fraud, theft, and criminal trickery in high places, even in President Richard Nixon's White House. Fusion musicians imbibed influences from all types of music—foreign, classical, rock and roll, even Indian music, and some African and Latin American music, too. Every type of sound seemed to serve as an inspiration for fusion musicians—and especially for musicians in an experimental branch of jazz, the free jazz movement. The free jazz players experimented with atonality and cacophony in their spontaneous, collectively improvised groups.

ACOUSTIC JAZZ IN THE 1980S AND 1990S

When rock concerts, at which fusion artists appeared, became dangerous by the end of the 1970s young people turned to videos for entertainment. Older people returned to acoustic jazz. And when long-playing records were abandoned in favor of new technology—compact discs—jazz fans bought the CDs to replace cassettes and records and built up new jazz collections.

Trumpeter Wynton Marsalis became a superstar. Recording companies began signing many young talented acoustic jazz players. In this atmosphere, guitarists—many of whom began as rhythm and blues players—turned to playing acoustic jazz, thrilled that they could now earn a living as acoustic players and even become leaders in traditional, mainstream jazz groups.

Emily Remler

Among them have been **Emily Remler, Mark Whitfield, Peter Bernstein, Ron Affif, John Pizzarelli, Jr., Russell Malone, Kevin Eubanks** and **Howard Alden**, to name a few. All of them found opportunites to play, as leaders and accompanists, in the most famous clubs, concert halls, jazz festivals, television and movie studios.

CHAPTER SEVEN

The Heirs of Charlie Christian Expand on the Innovations

After Charlie Christian, the most famous names in the jazz guitar world were Oscar Moore, already discussed for his role in the Nat King Cole trio, and Barney Kessel, Herb Ellis, and Remo Palmier, who played on one of the first Charlie "Bird" Parker-Dizzy Gillespie recordings. All these players showed the influence of the saxophonists—not just of Bird, but also of Lester Young, whose soft-toned, introspective sound and long, fluid lines heralded the bebop revolution in the 1930s.

Furthermore, as we noted in chapter one, rhythm sections in the 1930s didn't need a rhythm guitar player anymore. And the basic rhythmic unit changed from the quarter note to the eighth note. Guitarists had broader horizons.

By the late 1940s, another major developer came along—Jimmy Raney. Extending the ideas and accomplishments of Charlie Christian, Raney truly applied the harmonic and rhythmic innovations of Bird,

Dizzy, and the pianists Thelonious Monk and Lennie Tristano to the guitar. Raney also used techniques taken from European compositions to construct his solos. In the early to mid-1950s, Raney influenced many of his contemporaries—among them Tal Farlow, Johnny Smith, Sal Salvador, Billy Bauer, and Mundell Lowe.

Also in these years—the late 1940s into the 1950s—Irving Ashby, Chuck Wayne, and John Collins ranked among the better-known players. And a woman, Mary Osborne, made her mark, too.

JIMMY RANEY

Born on August 20, 1927, in Louisville, Kentucky, Jimmy began playing guitar as a little boy, encouraged by his mother. By age thirteen, he had a teacher who introduced him to the recordings of Charlie Christian. A few years later, Raney was playing professionally in local bands and

Jimmy Raney

determined to make jazz guitar his career. At eighteen, he was working in a New York band, where he became friends with the pianist Al Haig. Haig would become a prominent figure in the jazz world.

Moving to Chicago in the mid-1940s, Raney continued to develop, playing with various groups and budding musicians. Drummer Tiny Kahn recommended Raney to Woody Herman, a prominent big-band leader. In Herman's Herd, Raney played with saxophonists Stan Getz and Serge Chaloff. In 1949, Raney went to live in New York, where his friends were guitarists Tal Farlow and Sal Salvador, among other instrumentalists. And Raney became enamored of the beboppers there, particularly alto saxophonist Charlie "Bird" Parker. Raney was also a great student of Lester Young, the tenor saxophonist, who inspired many of Raney's lines and perhaps his coolness, too. Raney played with many musicians who were becoming well known, including Stan Getz again, with whom Raney recorded in the early 1950s. Then Raney toured in Europe with Red Norvo's group and followed that job with a gig accompanying Billie Holiday. He was voted Best Jazz Guitarist in several magazine polls by critics in 1954 and 1955. But, finding travel very distasteful, he decided to stay home with his wife and children in New York. He took up residence in a fashionable club called the Blue Angel on Manhattan's Upper East Side.

Raney worked in a variety of formats—Broadway shows, radio and television studios, and clubs, recording under his own name and with other leading jazz artists. But he found the jazz life insecure for his financial needs. He began to study the cello and composition and worked as an accompanist for leading pop and jazz singers.

In the 1960s, Raney went back to live in Louisville, where he remained until the mid-1970s. Then he began playing in clubs, making recordings, and touring with his son Doug, a fine guitarist, and his friend Al Haig. Eventually, Raney retired for health reasons. But among guitarists, his influence was far-reaching; they admired his flawless technique, his single-note playing, his long, melodic lines, his clean, articulate sound, and his creativity as an improviser.

BARNEY KESSEL

With no encouragement from his non-musical family, Barney Kessel, born on October 17, 1923, in Muskogee, Oklahoma, set his heart on playing guitar and bought himself an instrument with money he earned at odd jobs. At age fourteen, he was playing in an all-black jazz group in Muskogee; two years later, Charlie Christian, visiting his family in Oklahoma, made a special trip to hear Kessel play. Christian's attention encouraged Kessel more than ever.

By 1942, he was in Los Angeles, where he worked as a dishwasher but soon made his talents known in the jazz world. Critic Leonard Feather told how Barney, only sixteen when he went to Los Angeles, got a call by accident from band leader Ben Pollack. Pollack was actually looking for a guitarist who had previously had Barney's phone number.[1] So Kessel started playing in a band led by drummer Ben Pollack and starring Chico Marx of the famous Marx Brothers comedy group.

Soon Kessel was playing regularly on radio and in film studios. A historic, short documentary called *Jammin' the Blues* featured him in 1944. In 1945, Kessel led recording groups with pianist Dodo Marmarosa and saxophonist Herbie Steward and recorded as a sideman with beboppers Charlie Parker, trumpeter Howard McGhee, saxophonist Wardell Gray, and others. He joined several famous big bands—one led by saxophonist Charlie Barnet, another by clarinetist Artie Shaw—and toured with a Jazz at the Philharmonic unit that included Charlie Parker and Sarah Vaughan. With his fleet hands, great musicality, and versatility, Kessel attracted praise in bebop circles.

In 1952, he was invited to join the illustrious trio of pianist Oscar Peterson and tour again with Norman Granz's production, Jazz at the Philharmonic, which took Kessel around the United States and on to Europe. This job gave him greater exposure than he had ever enjoyed before. He won important jazz polls, including those of *Esquire* magazine (1947), *Down Beat* readers' poll (1956–1959), the *Metronome* magazine readers' poll (1958–1960), and a *Playboy* readers' poll (1957–1960).

In 1953, Kessel began leading his own groups on long-playing recordings, and later on CDs. He also helped popularize the guitar, bass, and drum trio format. He not only played as a brilliant soloist with many of the best instrumentalists of the century, among them guitarists Herb Ellis, Charlie Byrd, and Tal Farlow, but was also recognized for his accompaniment for the leading jazz singers of the century—Billie Holiday, Sarah Vaughan, Anita O'Day, and Ella Fitzgerald. He recorded with Benny Goodman in 1958. And, continuing as a studio player, Kessel played on the soundtrack for several Elvis Presley films.

In 1968, he toured in Europe with George Wein's All Stars. Wein had founded the pioneering Newport Jazz Festival in Rhode Island in 1954. By the next year, Kessel was devoting himself entirely to the jazz world and had become a prominent leader. He also taught students and wrote for leading magazines.

In 1973, with Charlie Byrd and Herb Ellis, Kessel formed a group called Great Guitars, a quintet with a double bass and drums, that performed and recorded for many years. A smooth and immaculate technician—qualities required of a studio player—this versatile guitarist can also swing hard and improvise jazz melodies.

HERB ELLIS

Herb Ellis was born on August 4, 1921, in blues country, in Farmersville, a small town in Texas, and the music of this region left its mark on his sound. By the time he was ten, he was playing the guitar, having already tried the banjo and harmonica. He studied at one of the first schools in the country to have a jazz department—North Texas State College—where he became friends with several other budding jazz musicians. In the swing era's early to mid-1940s, he played with big bands led by Glen Gray and Jimmy Dorsey.

Then Ellis played with the Softwinds, his own instrumental and vocal trio, for about five years. During that time he wrote several enduring tunes including "Detour Ahead" and "I Told You I Love You, Now Get Out." A crucial boost for his career came when he replaced Barney Kessel in Oscar Peterson's trio from 1953 to 1958. He became a close friend and colleague of Peterson's bassist, Ray Brown. Ellis then played regularly as accompanist for Ella Fitzgerald, the First Lady of Song.

Like Kessel, Ellis has played in the Los Angeles studios as a much-admired guitarist, as he was for his work in the Great Guitars group and in duos with Joe Pass, one of the great guitarists of the century. Ellis recorded with Pass and led his own small groups.

REMO PALMIER

Born on March 29, 1923, in New York City, Palmier began playing the guitar professionally to pay for art lessons. But he became permanently sidetracked by jazz when he heard bandleader Tommy Dorsey's recordings in 1938 and went on to listen to Django and Christian. By the 1940s, he was studying music seriously, and he soon developed a reputation as an heir to Charlie Christian.

Palmier's career progressed as he played with Coleman Hawkins, whose groups provided first-rate showcases for emerging talents. Palmi-

Remo Palmier

er also accompanied singers Billie Holiday and Mildred Bailey, and he performed regularly in the Phil Moore band at Cafe Society, the first racially integrated downtown jazz club in New York. In 1945, he won a New Star Award from *Esquire* magazine, then a Silver Award from that magazine the next year. He also recorded *Groovin' High* and *All the Things You Are* with Dizzy Gillespie for the Musicraft label. He then spent many years in the studios of CBS and NBC.

Though his first influences were Christian and Django, as time went on he also showed the effects of his admiration for the melodic and harmonic concepts of Hawkins and Charlie Parker. Palmier curtailed his jazz work in favor of studio work because of his health. He contracted pneumonia, and his doctor told him to take it easy. For twenty-seven years, he played guitar in the band for the popular show starring Arthur Godfrey.

From the 1970s on, Palmier divided his time between the jazz world and the studios. In 1975, he played in the Concord Jazz Festival's Guitar Explosion with Herb Ellis, Tal Farlow, Barney Kessel, newcomer Emily Remler, and others. He also appeared with Benny Goodman and the influential, multifaceted pianist Dick Hyman in the 1970s. In 1985, Palmier worked with his old friend, Red Norvo—a vibraphonist who had once been married to Mildred Bailey—and drummer Louie Bellson and others at an acclaimed concert in New York.

TAL FARLOW

Farlow experimented with several instruments until he heard Charlie Christian's recordings in the late 1930s, and then Tal began to play the guitar, teaching himself Christian's music note for note. Born on June 7, 1921, Farlow remained an amateur musician until 1943, when he was hired to play for USO dances at a U.S. Air Force base in Greensboro, North Carolina, his hometown.

There he met the jazz pianist Jimmy Lyons, and Farlow's connections and rise in the jazz world began. He played with Dardanelle, a pianist, vibist, and singer, in Baltimore, Philadelphia, and at the famous Copacabana nightclub in New York. He went to the 52nd Street jazz

Tal Farlow (left) with Charlie Mingus (center) and Red Norvo (right)

clubs and heard the great modern jazz musicians—Charlie Parker, Art Tatum, Erroll Garner, and Dizzy Gillespie. Other musicians would one day try to analyze who were the biggest influences on tall, lanky Farlow—horn players or Art Tatum. Farlow synthesized the work of the great players on many instruments to build his virtuosity on guitar.

His next major job was with the peerless jazz clarinetist Buddy DeFranco. Then guitarist Mundell Lowe, leaving Red Norvo's group, recommended that Norvo hire Farlow. Charlie Mingus, a titan among bassists, soon joined Norvo's group, and that trio's recordings became best-sellers among Farlow's much-admired recordings of the 1950s. Farlow became noted for his technique, brilliant improvisations, and original musical ideas. He played an electric instrument with a finger board more than 1 inch (2.5 cm) shorter than the standard pattern to achieve an individual sound. He developed a technique that made it sound as if a group had a drummer. "One such technique was to play chords [while] . . . tapping out rhythms on the guitar body and strings with his finger-tips."[2]

In 1954, Farlow won a *Down Beat* magazine award and in 1956 the *Down Beat* critics' poll. He signed with the Verve recording label and made several records with top-notch musicians such as bassist Ray Brown and drummers Chico Hamilton and Stan Levey. But Tal remained very down-to-earth. Guitarist Joe Puma recalled playing in a group opposite Farlow at the Composer club in 1955 on Manhattan's Upper East Side. Puma was intimidated by Farlow's abilities with harmonies and chords (though Puma himself was a noted player).

"I spent most of those two weeks just trying to get through my own set, then listening to him play . . . Tal proved to be an inspiration," Puma said.[3] One night, arriving late for his job, Puma was searching for a parking space. Farlow took the keys and parked Puma's Volkswagen. Puma was very grateful—and forever puzzled about how Farlow ever fit himself into that little car.

In the late 1950s, Farlow married and began to withdraw from the playing scene, retiring to a house on the New Jersey coast. After that he rarely ventured out to play in public. He was the subject of a video called *Talmadge Farlow* made by Stutz Cinema Ventures. He toured in Europe with Red Norvo and played at the Nice Jazz Festival in 1984, but he never came out of seclusion for long. His recordings, however, are readily available in stores.

Farlow was celebrated by his fellow guitarists at such events as a concert in 1991 at the Count Basie Theater in Red Bank, New Jersey, and a seventy-fifth birthday celebration at Lincoln Center's Merkin Concert Hall in June 1996. He was especially praised for his use of harmonics—the way he touched the strings at certain points and produced overtones, his ability to play at very fast tempos, the rapid flow of his ideas, and the unusual intervals (spaces between notes) in his improvisations. A quiet man with many contradictions, he was sometimes called a fiery player, and yet he had a gentle touch. He was also noted for inventing musical gadgets to enhance his playing and aid in his experimentations. He died in 1998.

JOHNNY SMITH

Because he retired from leading his own group on the East Coast playing scene in 1957, when he was only thirty-five years old, Smith did not attain lasting fame with the general public. But his fellow guitarists acknowledged him as one of the foremost electric guitar players.

Johnny was born in Birmingham, Alabama, on June 25, 1922, and later moved to Maine with his family. The son of a musician, Johnny became a multi-instrumentalist at a young age and settled on the guitar by the time he was thirteen. He began working in Portand, Maine, and Boston, Massachusetts. After a stint in the U.S. Air Force Band in the 1940s, he headed for New York City and became an NBC staff musician.

Smith won international prominence in the 1950s when he joined Stan Getz's quintet, and with his own group he recorded "Moonlight in Vermont," a hit and a classic of the "cool jazz" school. That happened after the hot, frenetic pace of the bebop movement spawned several new styles based on bebop innovations. In 1952, *Down Beat* magazine called "Moonlight in Vermont" the jazz record of the year. The next year, Johnny recorded on a Decca album, *Jazz Studio*, with pianist Hank Jones, drummer Kenny Clarke, and others. Johnny was known for his single-note playing and unique chord voicings.

In the 1950s, he played in East Coast groups, performing regularly at New York's Birdland, the most illustrious jazz club in the world at that time. He became associated with the Guild Guitar Company, then the Gibson Guitar Company, which named one of its most popular jazz archtop models after him. But when his wife died in 1957, Johnny took his four-year-old daughter to live in Colorado Springs, Colorado, and opened a guitar shop there. Singer Bing Crosby, a lover of fine guitarists, took Johnny on a concert tour in 1977—after Smith's daughter had grown up.

Sal Salvador

Sal Salvador, born in Monson, Massachusetts, on November 21, 1925, became intrigued with jazz when he heard Charlie Christian's records. When he was nearly twenty-five, he moved to New York and worked with influential musicians, including guitarist Mundell Lowe. Sal led his own groups and big bands and went on to head the guitar department at the University of Bridgeport, Connecticut. He has written several books on playing guitar.

Billy Bauer was born in New York on November 14, 1915. He loved Charlie Christian's work, played in Woody Herman's renowned first Herd band from 1944 to 1946, then went on to perform with bassist

Chubby Jackson, Benny Goodman, and trombonist Jack Teagarden, heroes of the swing era. Bauer's most creative period came in the late 1940s, when he joined pianist Lenny Tristano's groups and advanced from a rhythm guitarist to a bebop stylist. He even experimented with free jazz concepts. In 1949 and 1950, *Down Beat* gave him awards; from 1949 to 1954, he won the jazz guitarist poll in *Metronome* magazine. And between 1947 and 1953 he recorded with the Metronome All Stars in bands that included Bird, Dizzy, Tristano, Miles Davis, and trumpeter Fats Navarro.

He played on NBC's staff orchestra, taught at the New York Conservatory of Modern Music in the early 1950s, and performed frequently with the daring alto saxophonist Lee Konitz in the late 1950s and 1960s. Bauer lives in New York state and has spent the later years of his career working as a freelancer and a teacher.

Mundell Lowe, a handsome man who looks like an archetypical Midwesterner, was born on April 21, 1922, in Laurel, Missouri, and left home early—perhaps as early as fourteen—to play guitar professionally around New Orleans. His father, a Baptist minister, brought him home. But Mundell soon left to go back on the road.

From time to time, he returned home to his father, but for the most part, he spent his early years touring in the South, until he joined the army in 1943. His path crossed that of another soldier's—talent scout John Hammond—and Hammond helped Lowe get a job with drummer Ray McKinley's band in 1945.

After that, Lowe freelanced with important musicians in New York clubs and studios. He studied composing with Hall Overton, a classical musician with a special love for and understanding of jazz, and worked in the Sauter Finegan orchestra which had fine, complex arrangements.

By the mid-1960s, Mundell decided to move to Los Angeles, where he found many opportunities as a composer and arranger for film, television, and radio. He became music director of the Monterey Jazz Festival in 1983, after playing guitar in the festival for many years. He also taught composition for film at the highly respected Dick Grove School of Music in Los Angeles. He has been playing, touring, and teaching throughout his career.

Mundell's Roulette recordings with Sarah Vaughan and George Duvivier are among the true jazz classics. A polished, swinging musician influenced by Charlie Christian and then Jimmy Raney, Mundell belongs to the cool school of jazz guitarists.

Irving Ashby, who followed Oscar Moore into Nat King Cole's trio and then played with Oscar Peterson's trio, had a swinging style with a lively, bluesy underpinning. Though less of a virtuoso player than Oscar Moore, Ashby was a versatile accompanist with a good feeling for popular music.

Chuck Wayne, who taught at the New England Conservatory, had an eminent career as a player. He was Tony Bennett's arranger and music director in the 1950s. He also worked as an accompanist and sideman for Morgana King, Frank Sinatra, Dizzy Gillespie, Lester Young, Sarah Vaughan, and many others. And he played in the studios for the television shows of Merv Griffin, Gary Moore, Ed Sullivan, and Perry Como.

In his early years, in the 1940s, he was influenced by the warm sound and long lines of horn players, particularly Coleman Hawkins. In 1941, Wayne played with pianist Clarence Profit's trio, which became popular in New York at the same time Nat King Cole was struggling to become a star with his trio in California. After Wayne was discharged from the army in the 1940s, he played with Dixieland clarinetist Joe Marsala's band on and off at the Hickory House on Manhattan's Upper East Side and with Phil Moore's band at the racially integrated Cafe Society in Greenwich Village.

Wayne then became friendly with pianist George Wallington. Together they discovered bebop and found acceptance with its originators. Wayne played with Dizzy Gillespie in the group for Sarah Vaughan's first record on December 31, 1944. In the late 1940s, critic Leonard Feather called him one of "two or three top bop guitar men, deserving of much more recognition than he has earned."[4] All the beboppers were struggling then.

Wayne went on to play with high-profile groups—Woody Herman's Herd and then George Shearing's very popular quintet in the 1950s.

After that he worked with Tony Bennett, for Broadway productions, and on CBS television shows.

John Collins, born in Montgomery, Alabama, in 1913 and raised in Chicago, was hired by pianist Art Tatum in the 1930s. He moved on to play with leading young talents in New York in the 1940s and then won an *Esquire* magazine New Star award in 1947. In 1949, he participated in an important recording session with Tadd Dameron, in which Collins's guitar was featured as the lead voice with the horn section. The songs he played were "Focus" and "John's Delight" for Capitol, now reissued as part of a Tadd Dameron package on the Blue Note label. After Irving Ashby left Nat King Cole, Collins became the trio's guitarist for the rest of Cole's life. Noted as a wonderful soloist, Collins has led his own groups in the Los Angeles area, where he settled in the 1950s.

Mary Osborne, born into a large, musical family in Minot, North Dakota, on July 17, 1921, would later say, "I never had difficulty earning respect. I was never aware of any special consideration given to me because I'm a woman. Playing music was the most natural thing in the world to me. I did it my whole life. Everyone who came to my house brought an instrument. . . ." She strummed the ukelele at four and started playing guitar at nine. It was actually very unusual for a woman to become as accomplished a guitarist as she did. Because it took so much strength and stamina to play jazz guitar, it was considered a "man's instrument." And jazz was a man's world anyway, particularly in those days, when women usually neither qualified as musicians nor found themselves welcome in the all-male big bands living a hard life on the road.

But Mary Osborne was in love with her instrument. She memorized every note of Django Reinhardt's acoustic solos on records. Then she heard Charlie Christian in person. "It was like living through a bomb," she said about that event. "I stood there mesmerized. . . ."[5] The next day she bought an electric Gibson guitar just like Christian's.

In the 1940s and 1950s, she played with Joe Venuti, Russ Morgan, Buddy Rogers, and others, and wended her way with groups, some of them made up totally of women, to New York City. Because she could play so well, she worked on radio and in recording studios and clubs on

Mary Osborne

West 52nd Street, with Mary Lou Williams, Coleman Hawkins, and Duke's son, Mercer Ellington. She married a jazz trumpeter and led her own trio. When Django Reinhardt came to New York in 1946, he went to hear her on 52nd Street. In the early 1950s, Mary found a job playing every morning on a popular radio show. She stayed with it until 1968 when she and her husband moved to Bakersfield, California, with their three children and opened a guitar company. Occasionally she came to New York to play; the last time, she worked for a week at the Village Vanguard. Soon afterward, on March 4, 1992, she died in Bakersfield.

CHAPTER EIGHT
The Blossoming of the Great Individualists in the Late 1950s and Early 1960s

Building on the foundation laid down by their predecessors, a generation of great individualists blossomed. They were the giants of modern jazz guitar. The greatest of these was Wes Montgomery. Among his most lauded contemporaries were Kenny Burrell, Jim Hall, and Grant Green. Charlie Byrd, too, was an influential player of the era. He helped introduce the lovely music of the best Brazilian bossa nova players and composers to the American public in the 1960s.

WES MONTGOMERY

Wes Montgomery was born on March 6, 1925, into a very musical family; his brother Monk played both acoustic and electric basses and other instruments—vibes, for one—and his brother Buddy became a pianist. A late bloomer, Wes didn't begin playing the guitar until 1944, when he was nineteen and discovered Charlie Christian on records. Six months later, a club in Wes's hometown of Indianapolis, Indiana, hired him to play Charlie Christian solos. Wes also developed his own style, by means of his facility, technique, and inventiveness, and most important of all, his feeling—the seasoning, or gravy—plus a profound understanding of the blues. He played beautiful phrases with intense rhythmic drive.

Continuing along the path that Charlie Christian and his immediate heirs had blazed, Wes incorporated new developments in harmony and melody. And he took advantage of the ongoing improvements in electric guitars. Furthermore, instead of using a plectrum or a pick, he used his right thumb.

Wes's technique for playing octaves electrified his contemporaries and instructed every jazz guitarist for the rest of the century. From the very commercial guitarist George Benson to the jazz-oriented Pat Martino, everyone acknowledged an enormous debt to Montgomery. Wes wasn't the first to play octaves, but he made a specialty of it and did it better than anyone else. In the generation of mainstream jazz guitar artists who became well known in the 1980s and 1990s, Emily Remler, for one, learned from Wes's octave playing and adopted his technique.

Wes told Ralph Gleason, a fine jazz writer, in the early 1960s, "Playing octaves was just a concidence. And it's still such a challenge . . . I used to have headaches every time I played octaves, because it was extra strain, but the minute I'd quit I'd be all right. I don't know why, but it was my way, and my way just backfired on me. But now I don't have headaches when I play octaves. I'm just showing you how a strain can capture a cat and almost choke him, but after a while it starts to ease up because you get used to it."[1] He also talked about his thoughts on the use of his right thumb versus a pick or plectrum. His friends advised him to use a pick, because he could play faster and phrase better that way. But when he tried it, he didn't like the tone. He had to make a choice, and he chose the tone he wanted.

A devoted family man with a wife and seven children, he didn't drink or smoke. Wes really didn't like to travel. He worked by day in a radio factory, and in the evenings he played in the Turf Bar; when that job ended, he moved on to a late-night spot called the Missile Room. He may

Wes Montgomery

have had a heart condition—perhaps a heart murmur—from the time he was very young, but the exact problem isn't generally known. He certainly wasn't getting much sleep in those days, when he was struggling to support his family and play music, too. And he always loved to eat rich fried food, which wasn't good for his health.

For two years, from 1948 to 1950, he traveled with Lionel Hampton's band, but then chose to go home and play in little clubs again. He formed a quintet with some local musicians and recorded in groups with his brothers.

Cannonball Adderley, a well-known jazz alto saxophonist, was passing through Indianapolis and happened to go to the Missile Room and hear Wes. Cannonball called Orrin Keepnews, one of the heads of Riverside, a prestigious little jazz label in New York, and persuaded him to make a special trip to hear Wes, too. Keepnews had read an article by critic, composer, French horn player, and teacher Gunther Schuller in *The Jazz Review*, a little magazine popular in the jazz world. Schuller called Wes "a spectacular guitarist."[2] So Keepnews made the trip and signed Wes to a contract. With his trio, Wes made his first recordings for Riverside in 1959, *The Wes Montgomery Trio* and then *The Incredible Guitar of Wes Montgomery* in 1960—one of his most highly praised albums, now reissued as an Original Jazz Classics CD.

His recordings for Riverside generally are recognized as Wes at his peak. No effort was made to commercialize his music, and his sidemen included such pianists as Tommy Flanagan and Hank Jones, bassist Ron Carter, and drummers Albert "Tootie" Heath and Louis Hayes. Wes won *Down Beat* and *Playboy* jazz polls. In the 1960s, he traveled to San Francisco and performed with his brothers and with saxophonist John Coltrane. After returning to Indianapolis for a while, he toured again with his trio in March 1963. In 1964, he switched to a more commercial label, Verve, where his producer, Creed Taylor, gave him the backing of arrangements for big bands and string orchestras. His album *Goin' Out of My Head* won a Grammy award for 1965. Then *A Day in the Life*, an album he did for the A&M label in 1967, became the best-selling jazz LP of 1967. When he performed in public, however, he continued working with small groups. Among them were the fine Wynton Kelly trio with bassist Paul Chambers and drummer Jimmy Cobb. They recorded such classic albums as *Smokin at the Half Note* on the Verve label in 1965. The Wynton Kelly trio was terribly disappointed when Wes decided to leave it and work with his brothers again.

But Wes's homecoming was to be short-lived. According to most versions of the story, he died from a heart attack on an airplane enroute to Indianapolis, on June 16, 1968, at the age of forty-three.

KENNY BURRELL

Kenny Burrell, born on July 31, 1931, into a musical family in Detroit, Michigan, began playing guitar at age twelve. He would be nurtured by good teachers in public schools. And his own friends were fine, budding musicians such as pianist Tommy Flanagan.

First, Burrell was influenced by Charlie Christian and Oscar Moore and acquired playing experience in Detroit clubs. He also studied classical guitar for a couple of years and earned his bachelor of music degree from Wayne State University in 1955. Sometimes well-known musicians such as Dizzy Gillespie, passing through town, hired Kenny for gigs in local clubs. Also in 1955, Kenny was hired by Oscar Peterson to replace Herb Ellis for six months in Oscar's famous trio. He began studying for a master's degree. His mother encouraged his academic career. But then Burrell decided to try his luck in New York City.

Once in the Big Apple, Kenny found many opportunities to play and record with well-known jazz musicians—pianist Hampton Hawes, saxophonist Frank Foster, and trumpeter and fluegelhornist Thad Jones. Kenny also played with Benny Goodman's band in 1957. He was so versatile that he played in Broadway orchestras while maintaining a career in jazz. Other jazz leaders he has played with include John Coltrane, Gil Evans, Stan Getz, Billie Holiday, Milt Jackson, Quincy Jones, Yusef Lateef, Hubert Laws, Herbie Mann, Sonny Rollins, Lalo Schifrin, Jimmy Smith and Stanley Turrentine—all masters on a variety of instruments.[3]

Although enormously admired by other guitarists for his playing abilities, Burrell has been particularly respected for creating a prominent place for the guitar on the East Coast jazz scene, in the hard bop combos of the 1950s, after the bebop era ended. The hard boppers returned to the blues roots of jazz. They probably got their name, hard boppers, for the hard-hitting style of their leading drummer, Art Blakey. Other instruments were more popular in the jazz world than the guitar, but Burrell helped focus the public's attention on it. He often worked in guitar, bass, and drum trios, and he was successful in leading his own groups in jazz clubs, on recordings, and on tours.

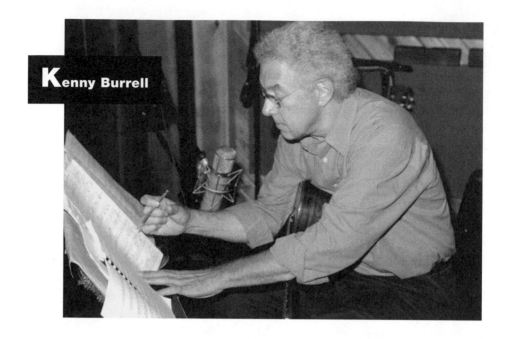

Kenny Burrell

Today, Burrell is a tall, elegant man with a mellow, melodic, sophisticated sound. He is as much at home on the stage of the Blue Note club in New York as he is as a professor in the music department at the University of California in Los Angeles.

JIM HALL

He is usually described as a sensitive, even delicate player. But Hall can swing and play with such strength that he can distract a listener's attention at times from the great tenor saxophonist, Sonny Rollins, on a song called "The Bridge." That was Sonny's famous album of the same title, recorded in 1962. Hall, as leader and sideman, has worked with many groups in many settings. That album with Sonny serves as well as any to illustrate the guitarist's powers as an accompanist and soloist.

Born on December 4, 1930, in Buffalo, New York, Hall led a rather unsettled life as a child. He was only a few months old when he moved with his mother and brother to Cleveland, Ohio, for a few months, then to New York, and then to Geneva, Ohio, to a maternal uncle's farm. Another uncle on his mother's side played guitar. By the time Jim's family moved to Cleveland, his mother and father had split up. For a while, the Halls lived in rooming houses while Jim's mother supported them with secretarial jobs. When Jim was ten, they moved to "a brand-new WPA housing project."[4] Jim was impressed because no one had lived in it before. His mother gave him a guitar for Christmas and spent a year paying for it.

Soon he was working in a Cleveland group, which had a clarinet player who loved Benny Goodman and played Goodman's sextet records for Jim. He immediately fell in love with Charlie Christian's music. Then a guitar teacher introduced Jim to records by Django Reinhardt. "Taking Charlie Christian and Django together, I've hardly heard anything better since, if you want to know the truth," Jim told jazz critic Whitney Balliett.[5] He kept working in groups, did well in high school, and went to the Cleveland Institute of Music. Halfway through his master's degree, he decided to leave behind the academic life, which he found stifling, and devote himself to playing guitar. When a musician with a lavender-colored Cadillac offered him a ride to the West Coast, Jim gambled on his talent. He knew he could stay with a relative for a while in Hollywood. Taking a job in a sheet-music store, he studied classical guitar and circulated on the music scene. In the time-honored fashion of the jazz world, he was recommended by one musician to another. Drummer Chico Hamilton, who was forming his own quintet to play music categorized as "cool jazz" and "West Coast jazz," hired him. The group had a laid-back quality that people associated with the dreamy, relaxed, beach culture of California. It was a sound that first became famous with the Gil Evans Miles Davis collaboration, *Birth of the Cool*, and then Gerry Mulligan's quartet including trumpeter Chet Baker and Chico Hamilton. The California sound in the early 1950s was, like hard bop, one of the major developments in jazz after the bebop revolution of the 1940s.

Not only was Jim suddenly earning $90 a week, he was lifted far up the ladder of the jazz world. With Chico, he went east to play at the Newport Jazz Festival in Rhode Island, then at New York City's Basin Street club. Jim met saxophonist Sonny Rollins, went on to saxophonist Jimmy Giuffre's group, and toured with singer Yves Montand, a great French music-hall star. From his perspective as a creative guitarist, Jim didn't like that job. He changed to accompany Ella Fitzgerald, the First Lady of jazz singing, on a tour in South America. But he stayed with Ella only until he reached Buenos Aires, where he quit to hang out with bossa nova players for six weeks. Back in the United States, he rejoined Jimmy Giuffre.

In 1959, Jim returned to the West Coast and played in a group with excellent jazz musicians led by classic jazz saxophonist Ben Webster in a club on the Sunset Strip. The next year, John Lewis, one of the founders of the Modern Jazz Quartet, a Third Stream jazz group combining European influences with jazz—the third major offshoot of bebop—called Jim to come back to New York and live in his apartment rent-free. Jim did it, gambling on his reputation to help him make his way in the jazz world. And he worked with excellent musicians once again.

Suddenly he began getting notes from Sonny Rollins. Sonny didn't have a phone, and Jim didn't answer his phone anyway. In 1962, Sonny came out of retirement, formed a group including Jim, and made a recording entitled *The Bridge*. The group played at the Jazz Gallery, a sister club to the well-known Five Spot. After several years with Sonny's group, Jim went on to another eminent group led by Art Farmer, a trumpeter, with bassist Steve Swallow and drummer Pete La Roca.

Jim was having a great deal of trouble with a drinking problem. So he joined Alcoholics Anonymous, married his longtime girlfriend, and went to work in the band for Merv Griffin's television show. It was a hard time for Jim, because he wasn't supposed to improvise in a studio band. He chafed at the constraints. On the other hand, by taking himself out of the bar culture and into a financially secure position, he was able to quit drinking. When he went back to jazz clubs after three and a half years, he drank only fruit juice and soda. And he led his own groups. So he climbed back to the top as a jazz musician, recording in duos and other formats with jazz stars—with pianist Bill Evans, for example, in 1966, and bassist Ron Carter in 1972 and in later years, too.

Still living in New York, Jim tours jazz festivals, clubs, and concert halls all over the world. He is celebrated and sought after as one of the greatest jazz guitarists in history, on a par with his idols Charlie Christian and Django Reinhardt. Full of admiration, guitarist Peter Leitch says that Hall always plays "the perfect note or chord at the perfect time in the perfect place."[6] And Whitney Balliett has written one of the best descriptions of any jazz guitarist's artistry:

> Listening to Hall now is like turning onion skin pages; one lapse of your attention and his solo is rent. Each phrase evolves from its predecessor, his rhythms are balanced, and his harmonic and melodic ideas are full of parentheses and asides. His tone is equally demanding. He plays both electric and acoustic guitars. On the former, he sounds like an acoustic guitarist, for he has an angelic touch and he keeps his amplifier down; on the latter, a new instrument specially designed and built for him, he has an even more gossamer sound. Hall is exceptional in another way. In the thirties and forties, Christian and Reinhardt put forward certain ideals for their instrument—spareness, the use of silence, and the legato approach to swinging—and for a while every jazz guitarist studied them. Then the careering melodic flow of Charlie Parker took hold, and jazz guitarists became arpeggio-ridden. [They played all the notes in a chord, and bebop was thick with chords.] But Hall, sidestepping this aspect of Parker, has gone directly to Christian and Reinhardt, and, plumping out their skills with the harmonic advances that have since been made, has perfected an attack that is fleet but tight, passionate but oblique. And he is singular for still

another reason. . . . Hall listens constantly to other instrumentalists, especially tenor saxophonists . . . and pianists . . . and he attempts to adapt to the guitar their phrasing and tonal qualities. . . .[7]

GRANT GREEN

Saxophonist Lou Donaldson brought electric guitarist Grant Green out of relative obscurity in his hometown of St. Louis, Missouri, and to the attention of the Blue Note label in New York. Until then, Green had recorded only with saxophonist Jimmy Forrest, composer of the hit song "Night Train." Green may also have played with trumpeter Harry "Sweets" Edison in the 1950s.

In St. Louis, Green began by playing in rhythm and blues groups. He also played in organ groups with such people as Jack McDuff in 1961 and helped establish the organ, guitar, and drums trio at a time when organ groups were becoming popular. Many guitarists worked with organists, because the voices of the guitar and organ sound fine together; their tones are compatible. And the organ plays the bass and keyboard, while the guitar, which can provide harmony, forms a good link with the drums providing rhythmic accents. The work of saxophonists Lester Young and especially Charlie Parker on recordings convinced Grant to play jazz in a style stressing long, single-note lines. Once Green got to New York and recorded for Blue Note, he joined the constellation of the jazz guitar stars. Hailed by critics, he recorded with a wide variety of people, including the organist Jimmy Smith as well as prominent saxophonists. With a strong blues influence in his playing, he produced fine, single-note lines with a very clear, bell-like tone to each note. His style was incisive and spare, with never a note too many in his songs. However, in the late 1960s and throughout the 1970s, he played in more commercial settings—rhythm and blues—and so he is not as well known in the jazz world as other great guitarists. Also, in the 1960s, Wes Montgomery's reputation in jazz overshadowed Green's and many others.

Green's health became shaky in 1978. He died of a heart attack the next year—at age forty-seven, his son Grant Jr. says—in New York City. But on his jazz recordings, his influence lingers on for guitarists, including the eldest of his four children—Grant Green, Jr.

Grant Green

Grant Jr. led a fine group at the Zinc Bar in New York in September 1997, playing his own tunes and his father's as an important part of his own jazz, funk, and rhythm and blues repertoire. The guitar-loving audience that frequents the Zinc particularly loved his interpretation of the funky "Cantaloupe Woman," which his father had written and played on his album *His Majesty King Funk.*

Grant Jr. at age forty in 1997 had poignant memories of his father. Following Grant Sr. around in his career, the family lived in New York, St. Louis, Missouri, and Detroit, Michigan. As a child, Grant Jr. began playing the harmonica, a gift from his grandfather, John Green, and then, at age twelve, the guitar, also a gift from his grandfather. Grant Sr. tried to discourage his son, hoping the boy would become a doctor or a lawyer. So Senior wouldn't teach Junior to play guitar directly, but Junior listened and taught himself. He knew how good his father's tone and phrasing were.

He also remembered how friendly other guitarists were. Kenny Burrell, George Benson, and even Wes Montgomery used to speak to each other on the phone. Junior admired his father's success with the pop-oriented album *Visions* in the 1970s. Grant Sr. kept playing more pop music and rhythm and blues after that. "It was paying the bills," Grant Jr. recalled of his father's direction.[8]

Grant Jr. began rehearsing his father's band for him. "I knew all his melodies," he says. He wrote a song, and he had the band play it in a rehearsal. His father overheard it and called out, "That's a good song. Whose tune is that?" A musician called back, "That's your son's!" After that, Senior started to let Junior, who was then twenty, play rhythm guitar in the band. "That's one of my fondest memories." Another time, Grant Sr. started to do that song in a Detroit club, and he forgot it; Junior had to sing the melody in his father's ear.[9]

Grant Jr. recorded *A Tribute to Grant Green*, then his own music on *Back to the Groove*, on the Japanese label, King, and finished a third album for Venus, another Japanese label, in 1997, just as he was taking a group equally gifted at jazz and rhythm and blues into the Zinc.

CHARLIE BYRD

Born on September 16, 1925, in Chuckatuck, Virginia, Byrd began playing the guitar when he was a child. By the time he got to France, where he toured with a U.S. Army band during World War II, he had a chance to play with one of the guitarists he most admired—Django Reinhardt. Byrd returned to the gigging scene in the United States. With his restless, inquiring mind, he decided to study classical guitar in the 1950s. He even traveled to Italy in 1954 to take a master class given by Andres Segovia, the great Spanish classical guitarist. Eventually, Byrd concentrated on playing jazz and popular music, using classical guitar techniques, including fingerstyle playing. He didn't use a plectrum.

Based in Washington, D.C., in the 1950s, he played regularly at the Showboat Lounge, in which he may have had an interest. He also played with Woody Herman's band and, on a tour with his own group sponsored by the U.S. State Department in 1961, Byrd became enamored of Latin American music. He picked up the idea to combine jazz improvisation and harmonies with the Brazilian samba. With saxophonist Stan Getz in 1962, he recorded the hit bossa nova record, *Jazz Samba*, and boosted both their careers. And so the Brazilian guitarist Antonio Carlos Jobim became one of Byrd's major influences.

In 1973, along with Barney Kessel and Herb Ellis, Byrd founded the group Great Guitars. A star and an author of instruction manuals for guitar players, he is perhaps still best known for his involvement with the bossa nova, for which he may never have received his just rewards.

His involvement with bossa nova began at the end of December 1961. Stan Getz was playing in a Washington, D.C., club. Byrd invited Getz to his apartment to eat lunch and listen to some wonderful Latin American music. Byrd had brought it home on tapes and records. Among the recordings was a jazz-samba hybrid called bossa nova. Byrd felt frustrated because he couldn't find a label to let him record bossa nova. He hoped that Getz, noted for his love of melodies, would want to record the music. Getz had more clout than Byrd with record companies.

Charlie Byrd

Sure enough, Getz fell in love with the tapes by guitarist Joao Gilberto and Antonio Carlos Jobim. "Despite the simplicity of the arrangements, [Getz] was fascinated by the limpid tunes and by the relaxed but insistent rhythm, which entered his bloodstream with alarming ease. Improvising over this, he thought, would be a pleasure; the rhythmic pulse carries you irresistibly forward, like a gentle wave."[10]

Stan told his producer, Creed Taylor, that he wanted to record bossa nova with Byrd. Taylor agreed, believing they might have a little commercial success. But Getz and Taylor couldn't find rhythm-section musicians in New York who could play the Brazilian rhythms. They turned to Byrd to organize a recording session with musicians in Washington.

In a book about Stan Getz's life, the biographer recounted Jobim's explanation that the words bossa nova meant "new flair"—since "bossa" means a "bump," which Brazilians used in the sense of a bump in the brain—or a talent or flair. To the samba rhythms, the Brazilians had added jazz harmonies and "recast" (the samba's) "simple, symmetrical rhythm into a subtle, asymmetrical one, which flowed hypnotically."[11] For their primary jazz influence, the Brazilians had chosen the American cool school. Creed Taylor, producing the Getz-Byrd album for Verve, on which Getz and Byrd shared the credits as co-leaders, decided to call it *Jazz Samba*. Creed didn't want to confuse the American public with the unfamiliar foreign words, bossa nova.

The album included five upbeat tunes and two more contemplative ones. The upbeat "Desafinado" and "One Note Samba" became the hits of the day. Byrd backed Getz with skill and exuberance on many tracks. The album received five stars—*Down Beat* magazine's highest praise in a review. Then *Jazz Samba* appeared in the *Billboard* magazine listings for pop albums in September. The song "Desafinado" hit the charts for pop singles soon afterward. Stan played selections from the album at the Monterey Jazz Festival in California with guitarist Jimmy Raney.

Afterward Getz played with Charlie Byrd on the *Perry Como Show* on national TV and then for a sold-out two-week engagement at the Village Gate. Stan was getting rich from the success. Other well-known musicians were releasing bossa nova albums by the fall. The bossa nova craze spread in the United States like a fire in dry grass. Getz went on to record more bossa nova songs with Brazilian musicians—Bonfa, Gilberto, and Laurindo Almeida—on separate recordings.

At the Grammy awards in May 1963, Stan won his first Grammy ever for Best Jazz Solo Performance on "Desafinado" from the *Jazz Samba* album. (The Grammy Awards are the highest awards given in the music recording industry.) Charlie Byrd was very unhappy that Stan hadn't shared that Grammy with him. And Byrd said he hadn't received enough money for the *Jazz Samba* date. Byrd told *Down Beat* magazine he had made the big mistake of doing the date and "not talking any deal. The next thing I knew, I was out. I mean, no artist royalty—none at all.

Just leader's scale, plus scale for the arrangements, all of which I wrote. All Stan had to do was come in and play. We had the rhythm section and the idea."[12]

Creed Taylor explained that "Desfinado" was nominated for Record of the Year and for Best Jazz Solo Performance. It won for the solo nomination. If it had won as Record of the Year, then Getz and Byrd would have shared the Grammy, but unfortunately Byrd's solo was cut out of "Desafinado" because of time constraints for the track. And Getz won alone.

The *Jazz Samba* album was still riding high at the end of 1963. The producers of follow-up albums done by Getz and the Brazilians didn't even release them for fear of competing with *Jazz Samba*. Charlie Byrd filed a suit against MGM, Verve's parent company, claiming that he was billed as co-leader on the LP and was entitled to a portion of the royalties. His case was weakened by his lack of a written contract to that effect. The suit spent years going through the legal system. In 1967 Byrd was awarded about $50,000 plus a percentage of future royalties.

A year later, Wes Montgomery died. At the time, a virtual revolution was overtaking the guitar scene, with a proliferation of electronic gadgets, accoutrements, and sound enhancers. Their popularity was part and parcel of the ascendance of rock as the most popular music in the country. In 1969, Miles Davis would record with guitarist John McLaughlin on the ground-breaking albums *In a Silent Way* and *Bitches Brew*, the first fusion albums. And the loud experiments of the fusion guitarists would make the guitar the most popular instrument in the country, as guitarists ventured with their music far afield from the mainstream jazz world. Some guitarists involved in fusion are discussed in chapter ten.

CHAPTER NINE

The Post-Bebop Mainstream Players of the Late 1960s

The post-bebop mainstream players were heirs to all the great guitarists before them, starting with Charlie Christian. They included Joe Pass, Pat Martino, George Benson, Gene Bertoncini, Attila Zoller, and Peter Leitch. Each of these guitarists deserves special consideration, and each one sings and swings on his instrument in a different way.

JOE PASS

The son of a steelworker, Joe Pass was born Joseph Anthony Jacobi Passalaqua in New Brunswick, New Jersey, on January 13, 1929, and raised in Johnstown, Pennsylvania. The eldest of four children in a non-musical family, he heard a guitar in a Gene Autry cowboy movie called *Ride, Tenderfoot, Ride* and asked for a guitar for his ninth birthday; his

Joe Pass

father obliged him. Joe began picking up hints from neighbors. They taught him the chords. Then one of his father's friends, who played violin and saxophone, taught Joe to read a little music. Soon his life was revolving around the guitar.

The stores in Johnstown carried mostly records by Perry Como and other pop artists and some jazz instrumentalists. Joe was very excited by the Coleman Hawkins record of "Body and Soul" made in 1939 and some Charlie Parker records he heard by the late 1940s. But the stores didn't have many guitar recordings, only Charlie Christian and Django Reinhardt. Joe began trying to copy the horn players, while he played in a group with his father's friends. They were amateur musicians who worked as barbers by day and modeled their group, Gentlemen of Rhythm, after Django's group, using two guitars, a bass and a violin. By his early teens, Joe also played with other local bands at parties. Although he was too young to play in clubs, he managed somehow to tour with Tony Pastor's band and then with Johnny Long's orchestra.

Joe was influenced by Dizzy Gillespie, pianist Al Haig, and Stan Getz, whom he heard on records. He would say later that his guitar playing came mainly from horn and piano players. "In fact, I made a point of avoiding any guitaristic playing. There are certain things that are peculiar to the guitar that a lot of guitar players use—certain bending of notes, certain interval sounds, and rhythmic ways of playing that you could trace right through the history of electric jazz guitar—and I didn't do any of them. I played straight lines and horn-like lines, and I didn't play rhythm 4/4; I comped like a piano way back." He loved tenor saxophonists Lester Young and Don Byas, guitarist Barney Kessel and clarinetist/bandleader Artie Shaw. Later in his career, Joe began to listen more to guitar players, but he didn't overdo it then either, always preferring to listen to horns and orchestras. And he was mightily influenced by the people he played with in his hometown.

Increasingly drawn to jazz, he headed for New York City in about 1948 to join the scene there. Not only was bebop firmly established, but a number of bebop musicians were using drugs. Joe joined that drug subculture, too.

> I played with a lot of jazz groups, but most of the time there wasn't a lot of work. Most of the time I was just sort of goofing around, just being around listening to everybody play on Fifty-second Street—Charlie Parker and those. I would go out on the road and tour with different little trios and quartets when I needed the money. Then I'd come back to the city and hang around. Then I

went to New Orleans and did some playing there. . . . There was a long period of time where I didn't play. I got involved in personal problems, and I didn't really function as a working musician, fully. I spent so much time trying to get everything straightened out. It took me many years. . . . Oh, I worked in Las Vegas for a while, and I played with various kinds of show groups; that was just working. But I always played jazz, always played gigs somewhere I could play.[1]

His career was so hampered by his addiction—"It was a waste of time" he later commented[2]—that he even spent time in jail and hospitals. In 1960, he decided to enter the drug rehabilitation program Synanon. He stayed in it for three years. And he kept playing his guitar. By luck, Dick Bock, owner of World Pacific Records that had recorded Gerry Mulligan's "cool jazz" group, heard the Synanon group and arranged for Pass to make a recording with other musicians in the hospital. Called *Sounds of Synanon*, it surprised jazz critics and fans. They recognized what a fine guitarist Pass was. He won a *Down Beat* magazine poll as a bright new artist.

His career began in earnest after he left Synanon. He went to Los Angeles, where he began working with important jazz musicians in recording sessions. From 1965 to 1967, he toured with pianist and composer George Shearing and became very busy in the Los Angeles recording studios with such jazz musicians as Earl Bostic, Bud Shank, Gerald Wilson, Les McCann, Chet Baker, and Johnny Griffin. Among his fine recordings in this period was *For Django*.

But Joe Pass still wasn't really well known. *Down Beat* magazine ran a regular column called the Blindfold Test, in which prominent musicians were asked to listen to recordings and guess who the artists were. When Wes Montgomery took the test in 1967, he identified almost every artist on every record, including George Benson and Grant Green. But he couldn't name the artist on a World Pacific album—Joe Pass. All Montgomery could say was "I don't know who that was . . . but it was beautiful. In fact, I couldn't concentrate on who it might be because of listening to it! . . . I like all of it—I like the lines . . . the phrases, the guitar player has beautiful tone, he phrases good. . . . It's really together. . . ."[3]

At Donte's, a popular club in Los Angeles, Pass became a familiar figure on Mondays, the jazz guitar night. In 1973 he toured Australia with Benny Goodman. And that year, Norman Granz, the major jazz concert promoter who managed Ella Fitzgerald and Oscar Peterson, heard Pass play at Donte's. Accustomed to recognizing musical genius, Granz signed Pass to Granz's new record company, Pablo. Pass's first album, a solo performance called *Virtuoso*, won him recognition. He began to show up as a major force in the popularity polls. That album was the first in his series of *Virtuoso* albums. He would be compared to Art Tatum, a masterful jazz pianist revered for his technique.

Pass stayed with Pablo for the rest of his life. Throughout his career, everyone would marvel at the beauty of his music, with his easygoing pace and his tightly controlled technique, in groups and as a solo concert artist. The more he played solo, the more he developed. He tried to develop songs onstage, and he tried to change tempos and keys in performances. He liked the feeling and the communication with audiences that he got from pacing his programs instinctively. One night he might play a program of songs that sounded exciting to him. The next night he might feel they were not working. They were boring or lacking emotional impact. So he instinctively decided on the spot to play different songs.

Or he might find that the acoustics of a room, or the height of his chair, or the air conditioning blowing on his strings and making them tighten up, affected his sound. He was constantly adjusting to his circumstances. One time he was thrown off his stride because the stagehands had set up his amplifier on his right side. He always liked to have it on his left, because he listened to himself with his left ear.

Through his association with Norman Granz, Pass often played with Peterson and Fitzgerald, and with singer Sarah Vaughan, too, who recorded for Pablo. He also recorded with Count Basie, Duke Ellington, Dizzy Gillespie, Herb Ellis, J. J. Johnson, and Zoot Sims, among others. He recorded at least twenty albums under his own name and another fifty or more with other people. And no other guitarist ever toured the world to give so many solo concerts as Pass did. For his concerts with Ella, which were sold out, Pass received critical acclaim. No one ever had a negative word to say about his work.

He particularly admired Jim Hall, Barney Kessel, Pat Martino, Kenny Burrell, Tal Farlow, and Charlie Christian, and above all, Wes Montgomery as the most innovative and swinging guitar player. And Pass could play with a fingerpicking technique—all the fingers of his right hand—instead of a pick.

He didn't think many rock players could play very well, but he did tell about a couple of nights when he found himself in a blues-rock group. The players with him were pretty good, he said. "I had the volume up, and I was right there. The only thing I got out of it was excitement, and it came from the sheer volume. It got so rhythmic, so heavy and loud that actually it'd lift you right off the floor. By the end of the night I was so tired I said, 'I don't want to play in here.' "[4]

When he died in 1994, at the age of sixty-five, he was one of the most celebrated guitarists in jazz history.

GEORGE BENSON

Benson began as a traditional mainstream jazz guitarist but switched his direction in the 1970s. Then he became a very successful and wealthy popular singer who accompanied himself on guitar. His recordings sold in the millions. Some people have criticized him for his turn toward commercialism. But his story has a fairy-tale quality about it. Any guitarist who has struggled to make a living from little gigs can understand why Benson made the choice he did—especially since he remained an excellent guitar player.

Born on March 22, 1943, George first played ukelele, nurtured by a stepfather who admired Charlie Christian. By the time he was eight, Benson was working in nightclubs with his stepfather, singing, dancing, and playing the ukelele. At age eleven, he began studying guitar, practicing on guitars he found in his friends' houses. Then his stepfather made him an electric guitar. George played in a rock-and-roll group right away, and by age seventeen he was leading his own group. Listening to records by Charlie Parker, Grant Green, and particularly Wes Montgomery, George gravitated toward jazz.

At age nineteen, he was recommended to organist Jack McDuff, who kept George in his group for three years, while he gained experience. With McDuff, he went to the Antibes/Juan Les-Pins jazz festival in the south of France and also to Stockholm, Sweden. There George played with Jean Luc Ponty, a well-known European jazz violinist. Then Benson formed his own trio, which played in his hometown of Pittsburgh for a while, and later went back to McDuff, and on to record as a leader and a sideman. He was much sought after for his speed and agility on the electric guitar. Among the excellent jazz musicians he played with at that time were drummer Billy Cobham, Miles Davis, Herbie Hancock, trumpeters Freddie Hubbard and Lee Morgan, and Ron Carter—all well known on their various instruments. Benson was respected as a fine player in the jazz world. His admiration for Wes Montgomery was especially apparent in his playing.

George Benson

When Wes died in 1968, it seemed a sensible idea to the record-business people to try to promote Benson as a successor. Producer Creed Taylor, who had that idea about Benson, gave him the opportunity to record for the A&M label. Benson didn't have the success that Taylor foresaw, until 1976, when Benson's recording of *Breezin'* for the Warner Brothers label became a hit. More than 2 million copies of it sold worldwide. Influenced by his eclectic background—a combination of jazz, funk, soul, and rhythm and blues—Benson can play fine single-note lines and excellent chordal improvisations. He can also improvise as a scat singer in exact tune with the notes he plays on his guitar. The technique is called "playing in unison." Few musicians have mastered it to the degree that Benson has. The technique has the effect of amplifying music; Benson as singer and guitarist, playing in unison, becomes a human amplifier, thereby further amplifying his electric guitar, which is, of course, already amplified. Benson has also maintained his ties to the jazz world and sometimes plays with jazz musicians. In 1997, the owner of New York's Blue Note jazz club, whose company books jazz and related artists into the Japanese franchises of the Blue Note, revealed that Benson can command $200,000 for a six-day engagement there.[5]

PAT MARTINO

A direct heir of Wes Montgomery, Martino has developed his own style based on Montgomery's octave technique.

The son of a guitar player and singer, Pat was born on August 25, 1944, in Philadelphia and loved to hear his father's record collection of Eddie Lang, Django Reinhardt, and Johnny Smith. Studying guitar with several teachers, Pat began playing professionally in a rhythm and blues band when he was fifteen, possibly with the saxophonists Willis "Gator" Jackson and Red Holloway. In his late teens in the early 1960s, he joined organ combos led by Jimmy Smith, Jimmy McGriff, Jack McDuff, and Richard "Groove" Holmes—all well-known organists in jazz and rhythm and blues. He then went on to work with excellent saxophonists such as Sonny Stitt, a protégé of Charlie Parker, and John

Pat Martino

Handy, a teacher and composer based on the West Coast. With Handy, Martino, who is a strong, tasteful improviser, attracted critical notice in the jazz world.

By 1967, he was leading his own groups, with such sidemen as pianist Cedar Walton, bassist Richard Davis, and drummer Billy Higgins, themselves a well-known jazz trio. And Martino was recording on the Prestige label, impressing critics and gathering fans. He branched out from his obvious admiration for Wes Montgomery and the technique of octave playing to listen to other kinds of music — classical music, eastern music, and jazz-rock fusion. Fusion was beginning to reign on the popular music scene. A child of his times in which the horizons for the guitar were expanding with electronic inventions, he also experimented with unusual electronic instruments—a guitar synthesizer, for one, and, as the jazz rock guitarists Pat Metheny and John McLaughlin have done, with an electric twelve-string guitar.

Into the late 1970s, his career was gaining momentum. But he began to have dizzy spells and other alarming symptoms. In 1980, when he was only thirty-six years old, he had a seizure. Doctors discovered a brain tumor and an aneurysm. An operation cured these life-threatening problems. He took a year to recuperate. But another three years passed before he could play the guitar professionally again, because he had suffered some memory loss. To remember his music, he had to listen to his own albums. And he would always like to bring sheet music to the bandstands with him—just in case he needed prompting.

His recordings after his comeback proved he was still a major force in jazz, with a cool style, complex phrases, and exploratory instincts. He was devoted to playing jazz as art music, as evidenced on his 1995 album, *The Maker*, and his 1997 album *All Sides Now*. On that one, he plays with a variety of guitarists, from Les Paul to Mike Stern, on the Blue Note label. In 1997, he headlined in a New York City club.

GENE BERTONCINI

Gene Bertoncini and bassist Michael Moore have become well known for their work in a duo since the mid-1970s. They have developed a following in intimate jazz clubs and jazz-oriented restaurants in New York City. Describing the elegance of the duo's work, *The New Yorker* magazine's jazz critic Whitney Balliett wrote: "The Bertoncini-Moore duet . . . favors brevity, gracefulness, and subtlety. It has no show business; it celebrates music. It is harmonically up-to-date and acoustically old-fashioned. Neither man uses much amplification—and Bertoncini often plays an unamplified classical guitar—yet the two achieve a full sound."

Bertoncini writes many arrangements for the duo, borrowing heavily from classical European music and techniques. He devotes himself intensely to the duo format and handles the business and the bookings for the duo. Moore also plays in many other groups but has a special allegiance to his work with Bertoncini.

Balliett described Bertoncini as an amiable, self-effacing man with a soft, quiet voice, who lived quietly in a small, bachelor apartment on the Upper East Side. He had been born in the Bronx into an immigrant Italian family, who encouraged him to go to college. He studied architecture at Notre Dame University, then came back to New York where he played the guitar professionally. Right away his father gave him encouragement. Gene always felt grateful to both his parents for their support of his music.

Among his earliest influences were Johnny Smith and Chuck Wayne. Gene studied with Wayne, who advised him to listen to the great classical guitarist Julian Bream and to Wes Montgomery. Gene had already been working in studios and orchestras when he decided to form his own trio and take it into a variety of clubs, including The Embers, a fashionable Upper East Side supper club. He also worked with Tony Bennett, composer Burt Bacharach, Benny Goodman, and singer Lena Horne. Like so many other musicians, Gene began to realize his time with Goodman was coming to an end when Goodman started asking him if he was playing the right changes—the right chords.

At around that time, Gene and Michael Moore started playing together. The collaboration seemed to be working out so well that Gene turned down a two-week engagement with Lena Horne at the Palladium in London. He stayed in New York just to play with Moore in a club for $75. The duo has continued for years. Moore went to live abroad for a while, but he came home to the duo, playing especially often with Gene in a restaurant called Zinno's in Greenwich Village. In the summers, Gene goes to the Eastman School of Music in Rochester, and Michael usually goes with him. Gene teaches, and he and Michael always give a concert there.

Balliett describes Gene's style as unique, since he has not fallen totally under the spell of Charlie Christian or Charlie Parker or anyone else, and he draws upon a wealth of eclectic influences and ideas. He plays a classical guitar, using an amplifier only if he is in a very noisy place. And his style is easygoing and thoughtful, with a soft sound based on single-note lines, filled with rests and short, manageable phrases. Yet the duo swings, with a strong, emotional impact on audiences.

ATTILA ZOLLER

Zoller, who was discussed in the first chapter of this book, was born in Hungary on June 13, 1927, the child of a music teacher and conductor.

Attila Zoller

Attila survived World War II in Europe unscathed. After the war, having played a number of instruments, he decided to concentrate on the guitar. He moved to Vienna, then West Germany, and began playing with visiting American jazz musicians. Those connections led to his migration to the United States in 1959, when he was thirty-two years old. According to a story Zoller told his friends, he decided to cross the border out of Hungary during the Hungarian uprising. To elude arrest, he got himself very drunk, stuffed a second pair of pants in his guitar, and walked to the border. If soldiers stopped him, he would be obviously drunk and say, "Oh, I didn't even know I was near the border." And they wouldn't bother him, just a poor, drunk musician.

Zoller received a scholarship to the Lenox School of Jazz in Massachusetts and decided to settle in the United States. He began playing with drummer Chico Hamilton, then with flutist Herbie Mann, and went on to work constantly with pianist Don Friedman, in a modal jazz quartet. That group improvised on modes, or themes, a series of notes with a tonal center, instead of on chords, as the beboppers did.

He continued working with Friedman while playing in many groups with a variety of musicians, from the swing-era leaders Red Norvo, a vibist, and Benny Goodman, to singer Astrud Gilberto, to the contemporary, often experimental alto saxophonist Lee Konitz, a disciple of Charlie Parker. Zoller loved playing in both mainstream and avant-garde groups, and he recorded with both to critical praise. His exciting work in a trio led by mainstream pianist Kirk Lightsey in a New York City club in the 1980s was highly praised by critics. They noted Zoller's uncanny ability, with his strong, forceful technique, to keep pace with his equally swinging and energetic colleagues.

He invented guitar accoutrements—electronic pickups and strings—and designed instruments. Attila toured often in Europe, where he was more widely known than in the United States, and taught in a Vermont guitar school. Unfortunately in 1997, he became ill with colon cancer, and he died in 1998.

PETER LEITCH

Born in Ottawa, Canada, on August 19, 1944, Peter Leitch almost immediately moved with his family to Montreal, where he grew up. He wasn't interested in much of anything until his parents bought him a guitar. It took him a few years to become serious about music. At age sixteen, he fell under the influence of Wes Montgomery, Kenny Burrell, and Jim Hall, "his favorites,"[6] he has said, and Belgian Rene Thomas. He met Thomas in Montreal when that guitarist began a sojourn there in 1956. Peter also was influenced by Sonny Rollins's recording *Saxophone Colossus* and John Coltrane's *Live at the Village Vanguard*. The horn players once again found an avid student in a very gifted guitarist. In Canada, Peter often backed visiting American jazz musicians including Red Norvo, Milt Jackson, and Kenny Wheeler. An American pianist, Sadik Hakim, who was living in Canada, recorded with Peter as a sideman in the early 1970s. That recording focused more attention on Peter.

Thirty-eight years old in 1983, Peter decided to change countries for his art. In Canada he wasn't feeling the challenges he supposed he would encounter in Manhattan. New York City's jazz musicians are famous for their dynamism, inspiration, and creative communion as well as for their competitive instincts. Peter's music, which has a quiet, even occasionally pensive aura, is propelled by his complex, flowing lines and embellished with exquisite subtleties and improvisations. And he is at home in any tempo.

So he and his wife and manager, Sylvia Levine, arranged their papers, and Peter established himself in New York as a jazz purist on electric guitar primarily, but on acoustic guitar occasionally. "I hung out, sat in, and got to know musicians"[7] is how he sums up the way he made his arrival known to the city's fine musicians. In 1984, he joined the New York Jazz Guitar Ensemble, which recorded for the Choice label. Then he began recording for other labels—among them Criss Cross, Concord, and Reservoir, for which his 1997 album was *Up Front* with bassist Sean Smith and drummer Marvin "Smitty" Smith.

Leitch has led groups in major clubs — Bradley's and Sweet Basil. Befriending the best pianists in town, he became especially influenced by them. "I've always tried to get the contours and phrasing of the line across. Now I'm trying to play the whole instrument in a complete way," he says.[8] He worked on improving and deepening his playing and his comprehension of the guitar's possibilities. For pleasure and edification, he moves from composer to composer — Thelonious Monk, Wayne Shorter, and Thad Jones among them.

He has recorded as a leader and a sideman on many albums. He has produced several, too, including Benny Green and Mike LeDonne quintet albums for Criss Cross. On Sunday nights from 1996 into 1999, he led a duo regularly with such people as the fine saxophonist Gary Bartz in Walker's, noted as a guitar room in TriBeCa. He travels to perform and teach guitar workshops in the United States, Germany, Holland, Belgium, Denmark, and Australia.

C H A P T E R

TEN The Fusion of Jazz and Pop, the Free Jazz Guitarists, and the Neo-Classicists— from the 1970s to the Present

Since this book concentrates on the mainstream jazz guitarists, this chapter will only briefly discuss the jazz fusion guitarists. They play extremely electric music and became commercially successful with the ascendance of rock in the 1970s. The loudness of their music is its most revolutionary aspect. The louder the music, the more popular it seemed to become. The fusion players are also boldly experimental with electronic developments and accoutrements for the guitar and the guitar synthesizer. And they deserve a book for themselves. Guitar magazines constantly feature these players and their equipment.

THE FUSION OF JAZZ AND POP

The most important and influential players were those who first learned the history of mainstream jazz guitar and who obviously imbibed a wealth of other musical influences, too. They included John McLaughlin in the 1970s, Pat Metheny in the 1980s, and at different times in these years, Larry Coryell, John Scofield, John Abercrombie, Bill Frisell, and Mike Stern in Miles Davis's later group. Some of these players are discussed in the postscript that follows this chapter. Metheny is actually so versatile that he cannot be typified as a fusion player exclusively. He plays everything from European-influenced new music to free jazz to jazz, rock, and fusion. And he is very popular, with a great deal of recording company support. He has worked in very inventive directions with many popular jazz stars.

Actually, most of the jazz fusion players are multi-directional, and in the 1970s, when they stepped out front in pop music, many had a firm

Pat Metheny at the 1994 Grammy Award ceremonies

grounding in acoustic jazz. At the beginning of his career, McLaughlin, for example, was enamored of John Coltrane's music, with its torrents of notes.

Fusion artists became prominent, playing their own hybrid jazz style, at a time when jazz in general and the jazz guitar had lost cachet. A few musicians had fusion hits in the 1960s. One was Wes Montgomery's "Goin' Out of My Head." But Miles Davis is credited with leading the first real jazz fusion albums, *In a Silent Way*, then *Bitches Brew*, which has a song, "John McLaughlin," named for the album's guitarist.

McLaughlin had the unique experience of taking his few belongings with him from his native England to the United States, where he planned to try his luck. A few days after his arrival, he found himself working in Miles Davis's band, just as Miles was going for an electronic sound. McLaughlin's friend, bassist Dave Holland, already in the band, paved the way for McLaughlin to find a job. It served as his stepping stone to a wildly successful career.

The highly electric sound of the music gave jazz a new lease on life; 400,000 copies of *Bitches Brew* sold quickly, four times more than Miles's top figure for a previous album. And a new genre of music was born.

The major jazz fusion bands of the 1970s were led, for the most part, by the terrific musicians in Miles's *Bitches Brew* band. (Bitch, by the way, was a musician's term for a great player. *Bitches Brew* was improvised and shaped by many of the people who played on it.) John McLaughlin went on to found the Mahavishnu Orchestra; he called himself "Mahavishnu" at this time. Some reasons for its success were his musical curiosity and his ability to imbibe influences and outplay and out-improvise his rock competitors. And the sheer loudness of his music allowed young audiences to transcend the tension in their lives.

The top fusion players benefited enormously from the growth in electronics. Musicians could overdub and record tracks separately. And the electronic sound of the music became a paramount part of the new style. Gone, of course, for the most part, were the subtleties, nuances, and intimacy of the acoustic or amplified hollow-body guitars. Their sound was sacrificed for the excitement and commercial success of electronic music.

Fusion musicians could congratulate themselves for breathing new life into jazz by attracting young audiences. They overcame the art-for-art's-sake image of acoustic jazz as it became more sophisticated and elitist in the late 1950s and 1960s—especially with the advent of the free jazz musicians.

For a taste of the best fusion groups that included guitars in the 1960s and 1970s, listen to the Miles Davis albums already mentioned. Other great examples include any Mahavishnu Orchestra album, particularly *The Inner Mounting Flame*, on Columbia in 1972; *400 Miles High*, a 1974 album on the Milestone label led by singer Flora Purim and her husband, percussionist Airto Moreira, both Brazilians, with Milton Nascimento and David Amaro on guitar; pianist Chick Corea and his band, Return to Forever, on the 1974 album *Where Have I Known You Before?* on the Polydor label, with Al DiMeola on electric and twelve-string acoustic guitars—a bold bid by Corea to equal McLaughlin's success; and George Benson's 1977 *Weekend in L.A.*, on the Warner Brothers label, which shows off Benson's warmth and infectious melodic talent very well.

FREE JAZZ GUITARISTS

Predating the fusion musicians, alto saxophonist Ornette Coleman, pianist Cecil Taylor, bassist Charles Mingus, and keyboards player and orchestra leader Sun Ra were composing and playing free jazz in the 1950s. At first, critics called it the "new thing" and the "avant-garde." The music was a radical break from mainstream acoustic jazz. The pioneering free jazz musicians liberated melody from pre-set chord changes and fixed tempos, they created new song structures, and they accented and colored music or sounds. And they improvised spontaneously and collectively in direct opposition to the concept of the soloist dominant in bebop and the post-bebop styles. For the uninitiated listeners, the most important aspect of free jazz was its atonality. Some critics said at first that it sounded awful. It took a while for the important critic Gunther Schuller to give the seal of approval to free jazz. He said that form didn't necessarily have to come first. Form could be a result of the materials played.

Even with the critics' eventual admiration, free jazz musicians on all the instruments attracted only tiny audiences in the United States. They played their bold ideas and sounds primarily for each other. For them, the 1960s and 1970s were bleak. Their commercial failure stood out in sharp contrast to the success of the more elemental sound of fusion. However, over time, a few American guitarists would manage to build interesting reputations and careers as free jazz players. The most prominent was Sonny Sharrock. He unfortunately died rather young, just as he was about to embark on some major recording work. And James Blood Ulmer wended his way from free jazz, which he played with Ornette Coleman, to free funk, as a group leader with commercial success. In Europe and Canada, several guitarists became well known for playing free jazz. Almost none of them were recognized in the United States, with the exception of British guitarist Derek Bailey. Europeans who had lived through the calamities of World War II found the cacophony of free jazz more palatable and emotionally comprehensible than Americans did.

However, in the 1970s, several events converged to make a great difference for all jazz musicians—including the free players. The free jazz players began to modify their experiments. Audiences accepted some of the oddness of the free jazz sound.

And the free jazz players influenced most other jazz players, both mainstream and fusion. At the same time, rock concerts, which had attracted huge audiences, became dangerous, and young people stayed away from them. They turned to videos for entertainment, while their parents sought more sophisticated pastimes. Record companies went into their vaults and reissued great old mainstream acoustic jazz records, hoping they might find an audience and fill the void left by the end of the rock-concerts era. The executives were shocked and delighted to find that people bought the older music. In some cases, recordings that had lost money in the 1960s were now earning profits. Then Wynton Marsalis, a promising and handsome young classical and jazz trumpeter, signed recording contracts with Columbia. He quickly metamorphosed into

James **Blood Ulmer**

a major star with great appeal to audiences and critics. Young fans bought his records and went to clubs and concerts to hear him. Other record companies began signing young musicians on all the instruments, hoping to find more young Wyntons.

A technological advance gave the final push to the renewed public interest in jazz. CDs—compact discs—came out. Many consumers were delighted with the new equipment—and could afford to buy it. Some of them bought jazz CDs without even knowing the music on them was jazz. And they liked it.

THE NEO-CLASSICISTS

In the 1980s, a generation of serious musicians turned to playing jazz. Most of them had grown up playing rhythm and blues and rock and roll in the 1970s. Some guitarists among them could switch back and forth from solid-body to hollow-body instruments. By the 1980s, new stars on all the instruments were emerging in the renaissance of acoustic jazz. The guitarists were writing their own compositions, and they were studying and playing the repertoires and emulating the styles of the classic jazz guitarists, especially Wes Montgomery and his contemporaries and heirs.

Young guitar virtuosos have been focusing attention on the brilliant history of mainstream jazz guitar. They have also taken into consideration the technological, sociological, and emotional changes in contemporary society. Among the newcomers have been Emily Remler, Mark Whitfield, Peter Bernstein, Russell Malone, Howard Alden, Kevin Eubanks, Ron Affif, and John Pizzarelli, Jr. As acoustic jazz itself became more popular in the public perception, these players mastered their instruments to the degree that they could play in all kinds of groups. They could work as leaders. They could also play accompaniment as side people without interfering with group leaders, particularly with the pianists and the horn players. And these young players (with the sad exception of Remler) are building bright careers.

It's hard to choose from among these players and feature one over another. But here are a few sketches of the new generation. *Emily Remler*, born in 1957, graduated from the Berklee College of Music in Boston, worked hard to advance her playing, and caught the attention of a major guitarist who was passing through New Orleans. She was paying dues—struggling—on the jazz scene there. He introduced her to people at Concord Records, who signed her to a contract. She recorded for Concord for her entire, brief career in the 1980s, playing with many established musicians and blending very well, with great clarity in her style, in particular with the pianist Hank Jones, a master of harmonies. While touring in Australia in 1990, she died of a drug overdose. She was one of the few jazz musicians in the 1980s and 1990s to die that way.

She had begun using drugs as a teenager in a New Jersey suburb, before she became a professional guitarist.

Mark Whitfield, born in 1966 on Long Island, New York, played saxophone and bass before concentrating on the guitar. He studied at the Berklee College of Music in Boston, recorded first for Warner Brothers and then for Verve as a leader, having already been saluted as "the best young guitarist on the scene" by *The New York Times* in the early 1990s.[1] He has been influenced by everyone from the blues guitarists to George Benson—as well as by Charlie Christian, Kenny Burrell, and most of all, Wes Montgomery. And he has played with such diverse musicians as organist Jack McDuff, singer Cleo Laine, trumpeter Nicholas Payton, and saxophonist Branford Marsalis (Wynton's brother). McDuff nicknamed Whitfield "Popcorn," "because I played really fast, with my ideas jumbled together," Whitfield recalled.[2] He has refined his playing since then. One way he did it was to learn the words to the standards he performed, just as tenor saxophonist Lester Young had advised musicians to do many decades earlier.

New Yorker *Peter Bernstein*, now about thirty years old, has been playing his hollow-body Gibson ES-175 for years in many groups, many of them with his contemporaries, all rising stars. But he is especially noted for his work throughout the 1990s in the group led by veteran alto saxophonist Lou Donaldson on records and in clubs. The bandstand of the venerable Village Vanguard is a familiar haunt for Peter. At home as both a straight-ahead and soulful player, he has a superb tone and fluidity in his single-note lines. His first outing as a leader was *Something's Burning*, with a quartet that included pianist Brad Mehldau, bassist John Webber, and drummer Jimmy Cobb, who has been Peter's employer in the group Cobb's Mob.

A graduate of the New School's jazz faculty, Peter has been playing the same guitar, with few gadgets to amplify or alter his sound, since he was fifteen years old. He has stressed versatility to convince leaders to hire him, but his most important quality is the brightness of his music, which can give a lift to any group and mesmerize audiences. People fall silent to listen to Peter's singing, soaring solos.

Howard Alden, who turned forty in October 1998, was born in New-port Beach in southern California. He heard the popular fusion players in the 1970s, but "I was turned off. I didn't really like the sound of the guitars. I was interested in straight-ahead jazz," he says.[3] He began play-ing little gigs, even one in a pizza parlor. He loved Barney Kessel records and taught himself to play by ear. In his early twenties, he played for a summer with the veteran, swing-era-rooted vibist Red Norvo in Atlantic City, New Jersey, and by 1982 made his way to New York City. Sitting in with prominent musicians in clubs, Howard immediately made it clear how well he could play everything from traditional early jazz to main-stream contemporary music with beauty and fluidity. Soon he was included in fine groups. Singer Joe Williams, for example, happened to hear Howard sit in at a little midtown club and hired him for a glam-orous gig at Marty's, then a fashionable Upper East Side supper club.

Everyone recognized Alden's accomplishments—his swing, his tech-nique, his thorough knowledge of his instrument and his jazz repertoire. He has recorded many albums with a variety of players, from George Van Eps to reeds virtuoso Ken Peplowski, with whom Alden has special communion. He and Peplowski have often worked in a duo.

Kevin Eubanks, from a very musical family in Philadelphia, became heir to the leadership of the *Tonight Show* band for Jay Leno on NBC after Branford Marsalis left it in 1992. Born in 1957, Kevin went to the Berklee College of Music, as so many of his contemporaries did, and graduated with a bachelor's degree in composition. First influenced by John McLaughlin, he moved on to study Wes Montgomery and played with drummer Art Blakey's Jazz Messengers—a group that rarely used a guitarist—but Kevin's talents made him stand out.

He has played with other well-known leaders. A jazz fusion player, he switches from electric to acoustic instruments. He keeps his hands busy with jazz on the weekends and during gigs in New York City whenever he can get away from the Los Angeles television studio. Inter-viewed by phone by Gene Kalbacher, Kevin quipped, "If you want to appreciate jazz in New York, come live out here for a while!"[4]

Kevin Eubanks (center) with former NBC executive Warren Littlefield (left) and *Tonight Show* host Jay Leno

Ron Affif, thirty-two in 1998, has become a mainstay at the Zinc Bar on Monday nights, traditionally an off-night in New York. Once he started playing there, guitarists flocked to hear him, and some of them brought their instruments and sat in. George Benson used to show up fairly often. He made Ron so nervous that Ron said he finally "mustered up the courage to ask him why he was doing this to me. George said, 'Look, man, if I didn't like what you were doing, I wouldn't be here.' "[5] Among the others who showed up were Russell Malone, Peter Bernstein, Mark Whitfield, Howard Alden, and Rodney Jones. On one memorable night, all of them except Bernstein showed up along with Benson.

For his major influences on guitar, Affif picks "Django Reinhardt, Wes Montgomery, Joe Pass, Pat Martino and George Benson—and horn players and pianists for their long lines and guidance about where to breathe," he says.[6] Affif has recorded for Pablo and has quite a few albums available in the stores. He sees his future as a composer. "The most important thing to me in completing my creative journey is to record my own music. Why do 'Stella by Starlight' again when you can hear Joe [Pass] play it? I look at my heroes: Benny Golson, Miles, Bird, Trane. They wrote melodies that mean something. That's where my future lies."[7]

John Pizzarelli, Jr., son of veteran guitarist Bucky Pizzarelli, began his career with his father in a duo and with his bass-playing brother in a trio, too. Born in 1960, now in his late thirties, John also sings very well. With his engaging, relaxed singing voice and manner and guitar style, he began leading his own groups, starring in festivals, clubs, and concerts, and recording very popular albums. He is noted for his allegiance to the wonderful old music of Nat King Cole's trio, and he seeks out interesting songs from the repertoires of the best musicians of the century.

Russell Malone, born in 1963 in Albany, Georgia, grew up in a religious family. His mother played the organ and sang in a Sanctified church—a church noted for the rollicking, swinging rhythms of its music. "She could really groove," he says.[8] Everyone clapped in church, and one old woman beat the rhythms with a spoon on a pot, he recalls. He heard leading groups in gospel music. He also liked country music played on guitar. The guitar was always a dominant force in his part of the country.

At age twelve, he saw George Benson playing with Benny Goodman and decided that the guitar, which he had always liked, was for him. He spent money he earned from a job raking leaves to buy a Benson album. A friend introduced him to Wes Montgomery's *Smokin' at the Half Note* and *Boss Guitar*. Overjoyed, Russell wanted to learn more and got records by Duke, Coltrane, and Lester Young. Listening to records, he taught himself to play guitar. "Thank God I was blessed with a good ear," he says.

Soon he was sitting in at a Saturday jam session at a local club called the House of Jazz; at eighteen he was legally allowed to work there. But he wanted to be "a veteran road warrior," he recalls. In 1984, he went to

Houston, Texas, with an organ trio. "It got so bad that I called my mom for money to get home." Three months later, he tried his luck in Atlanta, where he discovered jazz festivals and musicians ready to help him develop, especially Nat King Cole's brother, Freddie Cole. Russell played in pickup bands with Little Anthony, Eddie "Cleanhead" Vincent, and Patti Austin in a show called *It Was Just Like Magic*, and even a gospel group. In 1985, on the advice of Branford Marsalis, Russell took a trip to New York to hear music. Then Russell went back to Atlanta. "The good gigs," he said, began when he sat in with organist Jimmy Smith and then went to Smith's hotel room to talk about music. Russell played "Body and Soul" and "Darn That Dream." Smith gave him advice about substitute chords. "It was great, man," Russell recalls.

A year later, in 1988, Smith's wife called Russell to play with the band. In 1990, bassist Ben Wolfe, whom Russell had met in New York, told him that Harry Connick, Jr., needed a guitarist for his big band. Harry, passing through Atlanta, went to hear Russell jam at a club. Connick was convinced, and Russell stayed with Harry's band until 1994. He was already recording as a leader and touring with his own group. His first album, named *Russell Malone*, and his second as leader, *Black Butterfly*, were out by 1993. He made an exciting impression on his first CD by opening with a fat, strong sound on a swinging "Wives and Lovers." His mastery of dynamics surfaced in his dreamy, poetic composition, "Invisible Colors," the album's second cut. "When I Take My Sugar to Tea" swung next—real pat-your-foot music, in a short, sweet arrangement. After a mellow, slow ballad, "It's the Talk of the Town," he played "St. Louis Blues" with the sort of twang that made bebop singer Eddie Jefferson's voice so distinctive. Russell can play with great musicality on anything—blues, gospel, popular standards, and even classical music. So he has joined the ranks of superb young players who have imbibed the history of jazz guitar and established themselves as polished virtuosos in the 1980s and 1990s.

In 1995, having moved to New York, saddened by the breakup of his marriage in Atlanta, he became known in the clubs as a musical force. He played with pianist Mulgrew Miller and bassist Peter Washington in

Bradley's, a leading jazz club featuring pianists for many years. Few guitarists got a chance to play there. Russell met singer-pianist Diana Krall at Bradley's. Her career was gaining momentum. She invited him to record her tribute album to Nat Cole. Russell has been traveling and recording with her since then, starring in first-class clubs and concert halls such as the Algonquin Hotel's Oak Room in New York and Lincoln Center, as well as in Japan, Europe, and Brazil. He led his own group at New York's great Village Vanguard club in 1998 and 1999.

In 1998, he led his own new album, *Sweet Georgia Peach*, on the Impulse label. He played on the sound track of the movie *Kansas City*. Constantly working, he practices for half an hour every morning or listens to music as soon as he wakes up. If he is playing at night, he usually goes out afterward to hear other musicians or to sit in with them. In short, he keeps himself immersed in music, and he doesn't let anything discourage or distract him. He had a contract with Columbia for his first two albums. "I know what it's like to be hyped and dropped," he says, referring to that contract, which came to an end after two albums. "I'm realistic. I want more experience. I want to play with Kenny Barron, John Hicks, Ray Drummond," he says about a few of the middle-aged jazz musicians dominating the art in the 1990s.

On his first album, Harry Connick, Jr., joined him and, at one point, enlivened the proceedings by calling out, "Play me some geetar!"[9] Essentially, that's what all these young virtuosos are doing, as they study their craft and develop their artistry. And they are bringing the amplified acoustic guitar fully into the limelight.

Postscript

The author wishes to apologize to many guitarists who were either left out or mentioned only briefly in this historical survey. One was swing-era bandleader Alvino Rey, an electric guitar player, who played rhythm guitar and added glisses and Hawaiian music sounds to his popular show band, playing arrangements by some of the finest arrangers in the country, in the pre-World War II era.

Others have been important jazz-rock fusion players and neo-classicists now making themselves known in the jazz world.

Among them are the versatile Joe Beck; Larry Coryell, one of the first fusion players, who became so ubiquitous that he is found on many albums; Eric Gale, who played on pop and r&b albums and was noted as a great studio player; Earl Klugh, a fingerstyle player with popular success, under the influence of the cool jazz guitar players; Al DiMeola, who has phenomenal technique; and Lee Ritenour, a very important guitarist in the Hollywood milieu. Those are some older players in fusion.

Among the younger players is Stanley Jordan, who has extended the technique of playing with both hands, tapping the strings with his fingertips on the fingerboard, as if it were a piano keyboard. Previously, guitarists used this technique solely for ornamentation, but Jordan does it as the basis of his style on the solid-body electric guitar; tapping out two different lines at the same time, he sounds like two guitarists.

Also in this group are Robben Ford, a founder of the popular group Yellowjackets; the astounding French gypsy guitarist Bireli Lagrene, whose recordings are readily available, and who has given concerts in the United States; and Hiram Bullock, whose career took off when he came from Florida to New York, became associated with saxophonist David Sanborn, began doing studio work, and played in Gil Evans's orchestra.

Mike Stern became prominent playing with Miles Davis. His wife, German-born guitarist Leni Stern, has become known in fusion circles. In 1998, both were leading their own separate groups in the 55 Club on Greenwich Village's Christopher Street. Bill Frisell, like McLaughlin, the poetic John Abercrombie, and a few others including Pat Metheny, plays both guitar and guitar synthesizer. John Scofield combines mainstream acoustic jazz guitar influences in jazz with a biting, blues sound; he also gained prominence in a Miles Davis group.

Fitting into no particular group is Ralph Towner, a contemporary improviser rather than a jazz musician, who was heavily influenced by European classical music. He played with the fusion group Weather Report and became leader of an experimental group called Oregon. He stresses his love for the piano, his first instrument, and plays classical and twelve-string guitars.

In the acoustic guitar world, Joe Diorio, Jack Wilkins, Gray Sargent, Bruce Foreman, Jimmy Bruno, and Vic Juris and the younger players Mark Elf, Joshua Breakstone, and Garrison Fewell are important players, whose recordings are available. And studio player, Phil Upchurch, can be heard on various important albums.

Source Notes

Chapter One

1. From the author's interview with Mundell Lowe in the early 1990s.

2. From the author's interview with Attila Zoller in the 1990s.

Chapter Two

1. Samuel Charters, *The Country Blues* (New York: Rinehart, 1959), p. 59.

2. Ibid., p. 60.

3. Ibid., p. 61.

4. Ibid., p. 62.

5. Ibid., p. 72.

6. Maurice Summerfield, *The Jazz Guitar,* third edition (Newcastle Upon Tyne, UK: Ashley Mark, 1993), p. 169.

7. Summerfield, p. 169

8. Charters, p. 207.

Chapter Three

1. Summerfield, p. 144.

2. Barry Kernfeld, editor, *The New Grove Dictionary of Jazz* (New York: St. Martin's, 1995), p. 450.

3. Nat Hentoff, *Listen to the Stories* (New York: HarperCollins, 1995), p. 197.

4. Summerfield, p. 104.

5. From Al Casey's eighty-second-birthday celebration broadcast on September 15, 1997, on Columbia University's station, WKCR-FM, hosted by jazz historian Phil Schaap.

Chapter Four

1. Marshall W. Stearns, *The Story of Jazz* (New York: Oxford University Press, 1958), p. 171.

2. Richard Hadlock, *Jazz Masters of the Twenties* (New York: Macmillan, 1965), p. 240.

3. Ibid., p. 241.

4. Bing Crosby, *Call Me Lucky* (New York: Simon and Schuster, New York, 1953), quoted in Hadlock, p. 253.

5. Leslie Gourse, *Unforgettable: The Life and Mystique of Nat King Cole* (New York: St. Martin's, 1991), p. 27.

6. Ibid., p. 227.

7. Ibid.

Chapter Six

1. Nat Shapiro and Nat Hentoff, editors, *The Jazz Makers—Essays on the Greats of Jazz* (New York: Rinehart, 1957), p. 322.

2. Ibid., p. 322.

3. Ibid., p. 323.

4. Ibid., p. 323.

5. Ibid., p. 325.

6. Ibid., p. 325.

7. Ibid., p. 326.

8. Ibid., p. 327.

9. Gourse, p. 16.

10. From the author's interview with Les Paul in New York, 1989.

Chapter Seven

1. Leonard Feather, *Inside Jazz* (New York: J. J. Robbins and Sons, 1949), p. 90.

2. Summerfield, p. 119.

3. Gene Kalbacher, "Tal Farlow," *Hot House* (June 1996), p. 21.

4. Feather, p. 100.

5. Jeff Levenson, "Mary Osborne," *Hot House* (August 1991), p. 14.

Chapter Eight

1. From liner notes by Don DeMichael for *Far Wes,* Pacifica Jazz, 1975. See the Suggested Listening section.

2. Summerfeld, p. 215.

3. Kernfeld, p. 171.

4. Whitney Balliett, *56 Portraits in Jazz* (New York: Oxford University Press, 1986), p. 344.

5. Ibid., p. 345.

6. From the author's interview with Peter Leitch about jazz guitar in 1997.

7. Balliett, p. 339.

8. From the author's interview with Grant Green, Jr,. in the Zinc Bar, New York, September 1997.

9. Ibid.

10. Donald L. Maggin, *Stan Getz: A Life in Jazz* (New York: Quill/Morrow, 1996), p. 207.

11. Ibid., p. 208.

12. Ibid., p. 218.

Chapter Nine

1. James Sallis, editor, *The Guitar in Jazz: An Anthology* (Lincoln: University of Nebraska Press, 1996), p.124.

2. Ibid., p. 126.

3. Leonard Feather, "Blindfold Test," *Down Beat* magazine (June 29, 1967).

4. Sallis, p. 133.

5. From the author's interview with Danny Bensusan, owner of New York's Blue Note, summer 1997.

6. From the author's interview with Peter Leitch in New York, 1989.

7. Ibid.

8. Ibid.

Chapter Ten

1. Gene Kalbacher, "Mark Whitfield," *Hot House* (October 1994), p. 21.

2. Ibid.

3. "Trad, Not Fad," *Jazz Iz* magazine (August 1997), p. 66.

4. Gene Kalbacher, "Kevin Eubanks," *Hot House* (August 1995), p. 18.

5. "The Gig That Changed My Life," *Down Beat* (May 1997), p. 56.

6. From the author's conversation with Ron Affif in New York City, August 1997.

7. "The Gig That Changed My Life," p. 56.

8. From the author's interview with Russell Malone in New York City, August 1997.

9. From Russell Malone's first album as leader for Columbia.

Suggested Listening

The author especially thanks Adam Valk, who works at J&R Music store and plays guitar with the rock band, The Want, for his advice about the following list. His group, a collective, has a CD, *Acid Millenium*, on the Mack Daddy label. New York, 1997. Note that for many albums no dates, especially reissue dates, are available. However, all CDs were issued since the mid-1980s.

Collections

Several collections and jazz-guitar group recordings have tracks by a variety of important guitarists, including:

Fifty Years of Jazz Guitar, various artists, 2 CDs, Sony Music Special Products, 1976. In this collection are Teddy Bunn, George Benson, Kenny Burrell, Charlie Byrd, John McLaughlin, Django Reinhardt, and Charlie Christian with the Benny Goodman jazz band.

Straight Tracks, the Great Guitars group, with Herb Ellis, Barney Kessel, Charlie Byrd, Concord Jazz.

Return of the Great Guitars, Ellis, Kessel, Byrd, and Larry Coryell and Mundell Lowe, Concord Jazz, 1996.

A Tribute to Wes Montgomery, featuring guitarists Tal Farlow, Herb Ellis, Jimmy Raney, Cal Collins, and Royce Campbell, Evidence, 1994.

Jazz at the Philharmonic: The First Concert, Verve. Recorded live at Philharmonic Hall on July 2, 1944, featuring an all-star group and produced by Norman Granz. The guitarist was Les Paul.

Robert Johnson
The Complete Recordings, 2 CDs, Columbia/Legacy, 1990.

Huddie Ledbetter (Leadbelly)
King of the 12 String Guitar, Columbia/Legacy, 1991.

Lonnie Johnson
The Complete Folkway Recordings, Folkway/Smithsonian, recorded in 1967; originally issued in 1982; reissued in 1993. Also see Eddie Lang.

Blind Lemon Jefferson
Blind Lemon Jefferson, a self-titled album, Milestone, 1992.

Big Bill Broonzy
Historic Concert Recordings, Southland, 1959.

Blind Willie McTell
Blind Willie McTell, 1927–1949, Wolf (an import from the United Kingdom).

Freddie Green
Count Basie's The Complete Decca Recordings, 3 CDs, Decca Jazz, 1937–1939.

Eddie Lang
A Handful of Riffs, AJA, 1989. Includes several classic tracks featuring Lang and Lonnie Johnson.

Masters of Jazz, Vol. 1, Rhino Records, 1966. Contains tracks by Lang with the groups of saxophonist Frankie Trumbauer, cornetist Bix Beiderbecke, and violinist Joe Venuti.

Joe Venuti/Eddie Lang, 1926-1933, ABC Music.

Oscar Moore
The Oscar Moore Quartet, VSOP.

Best of the Nat King Cole Trio, Capitol/EMI, 1943–1949. Contains tracks with Moore, 1943–1946, and Irving Ashby, 1947–1949.

Tiny Grimes
Blues Groove, Original Jazz Classics, 1958. With Coleman Hawkins.

Art Tatum's *Trio Days*, Le Jazz 43 label, originally recorded 1944.

Art Tatum's *1944*, Classics.

Art Tatum's *On the Sunny Side*, Topaz, 1944–1945.

Other Tatum trio recordings with Grimes are also always available in stores.

Eddie Condon
Eddie Condon (1938–40), a self-titled album, Classics.

Danny Barker
Save the Bones, Orleans Records, 1988. Barker was a noted New Orleans banjoist and guitarist.

Django Reinhardt
Django Reinhardt in Brussels, Verve, 1992.

Verve Jazz Masters 38, Verve, 1994. This one was recorded in a studio; he also has many live recordings, solo recordings, recordings with jazz violinist Stephane Grappelli and with the Hot Club of France Quintet, and gypsy music records. Many CDs by Django are available, and all of them are good.

Charlie Christian
The Benny Goodman Sextet featuring Charlie Christian, Columbia, 1939–1941.

Live at Minton's, Jazz Anthology, 1941.

Jimmy Raney
The Master, Criss Cross.

A, Prestige, now an Original Jazz Classics reissue.

But Beautiful, Criss Cross, reissued 1990. (On this he plays a Zoller guitar designed by Attila Zoller.)

Barney Kessel
Kessel Plays Standards, Original Jazz Classics, 1955.

Lester Young/Oscar Peterson, with the Peterson Trio (pianist Peterson, bassist Ray Brown, and Kessel), Verve, 1959.

Herb Ellis/Red Mitchell
Doggin' Around, Concord Jazz.

The Oscar Peterson Trio at the Stratford Shakespearian Festival, Verve, 1956. This is one of the best, if not the best recording of the great trio with Ellis, Peterson, and Ray Brown.

Tal Farlow
Chromatic Palette, Concord Jazz, 1994.

Verve Jazz Masters, Verve, 1995.

Billy Bauer
The Complete Lennie Tristano Keynote Recordings, Mercury, 1987.

Johnny Smith/George Van Eps
Legends, Concord Jazz, 1944. The Gibson company named one of its guitars for Johnny Smith.

Les Paul
All Time Greatest Hits, with singer Mary Ford, CEMA Special Products,1992.

The Great Artistry of Les Paul, One Way Records.

Les Paul invented the solid-body electric guitar and multitrack recording. He and his wife, Mary Ford, had major hits together in the 1950s, including "How High the Moon" and "The World Is Waiting for the Sunrise."

Wes Montgomery
Impressions: The Verve Sides, 2 CDs, Verve, 1995. Contains the complete classic album, *Smokin' at the Half Note*, on disc 2.

A Day in the Life, A&M Records, 1967.

Far Wes, Pacific Jazz. Includes performances by his brothers Buddy, a pianist, and Monk, a bassist, and others; also on Blue Note records.

Fingerpickin', Pacific Jazz, 1957–1958.

Also *Boss Guitar* and other excellent Wes Montgomery albums are available in the stores. Generally regarded as among his best is *The Incredible Jazz Guitar of Wes Montgomery*, on Riverside. All his Riverside recordings are recommended.

Jim Hall
Undercurrent, Blue Note, 1962. Includes performances by pianist Bill Evans.

Concierto, CTI/CBS, 1975.

Textures, Tel Arc, 1997.

Sonny Rollins's *The Bridge*, BMG, reissued 1996, originally recorded 1962.

Kenny Burrell
Blue Lights, 2 CDs, Blue Note, originally recorded in 1958.

A Night at the Vanguard, Chess, originally recorded in 1959. With drummer Roy Haynes and bassist Richard Davis.

Jimmy Smith's *Got My Mojo Workin/Hoochie Coochie Man*, Verve, 1997.

Guitar Forms, Verve, 1965.

Grant Green, Jr.

Idle Moments, Blue Note.

The Matador, Blue Note. With guest McCoy Tyner, pianist.

The Complete Quartets, Blue Note, 1997. With Sonny Clarke, pianist, Sam Jones, bass, and Art Blakey and Louis Hayes, drums, recorded in the early 1960s.

Charlie Byrd

Jazz Samba, Verve, 1962.

Joe Pass

Virtuoso, a solo album, Pablo, 1974.

Appassionato, Pablo, 1991.

Nuages, Live at Yoshi's, Vol. 2, Pablo, 1992.

Pass is also on many albums with singer Ella Fitzgerald and pianist Oscar Peterson, as well as other solo and group albums. The bins are filled with the work of this legendary guitarist.

Pat Martino

The Maker, Evidence, ECD, 1997. This was recorded in 1994.

All Sides Now, Blue Note, 1997. A new album with an all-star group, including Les Paul, Kevin Eubanks, Charlie Hunter, Joe Satriani, Michael Hedges, and Mike Stern.

Footprints, 32 Records, 1975.

Consciousness, one of Martino's best albums, is no longer made, but it will undoubtedly be reissued and made available soon.

George Benson

Breezin', Warner Bros., 1976.

White Rabbit, CTI/CBS. On this CD are Earl Klugh and also widely recorded East Coast studio guitarist Jay Berliner.

Earl Klugh

Sudden Burst of Energy, Warner Bros., 1996. This can be categorized as popular, contemporary jazz fusion.

Gene Bertoncini

O Grande Amor, a bossa nova collection, Viper's Nest label.

Bertoncini and bassist Michael Moore have done many duo albums. All of them are recommended.

Attila Zoller

Thingin, Hat Hut Records. With pianist Don Friedman and saxophonist Lee Konitz. This album may be hard to find.

Common Cause, Enja, 1979.

When It's Time, Enja, 1995.

The Horizon Beyond, the Attila Zoller Quartet, Act Music and Vision, 1992. A German import, this may not be easy to find, either. It is however very interesting avant-garde, experimental music.

Peter Leitch

Up Front, Reservoir, 1997.

Colours and Dimensions, Reservoir, 1996.

Duality, Reservoir, 1995.

A Special Rapport, Reservoir, 1994.

Portraits and Dedications, Criss Cross, 1989.

Leitch has also recorded three albums for Concord and two for Criss Cross.

Joe Diorio

To Jobim with Love, a tribute to the music of Antonio Carlos Jobim, RAM Records, 1996.

John McLaughlin

Birds of Fire and *Enigmatic Flame*, with the Mahavishnu Orchestra, are available in some stores, and other albums with that orchestra are also available in some stores. Also, McLaughlin played on the Miles Davis albums, *In a Silent Way*, Columbia, 1969, and *Bitches Brew*, Columbia, 1969. *Bitches Brew* contains a song entitled "John McLaughlin."

Larry Coryell

Spaces, Vanguard, 1970.

Together, with Emily Remler, Concord.

Kevin Eubanks
The Heat of Heat, GRP, 1987.

Also, he moved from GRP to Blue Note, where he made albums such as *Turning Point,* 1992, and *Spirittalk,* 1995.

John Scofield
The Best of John Scofield, Blue Note, 1996. Features guitarists Pat Metheny and Bill Frisell.

Liquid Fire, Gramavision, 1994.

John Abercrombie
Works, ECM, 1988.

Gateway, ECM, 1975. With drummer Jack DeJohnette and bassist Dave Holland.

Emerald City, Evidence, 1994. With pianist Richie Beirach.

Pat Metheny
American Garage, ECM, 1979.

Also see John Scofield.

Bright Size Life, ECM, 1976. Includes the great electric bassist Jaco Pastorius.

Ornette Coleman's *Song X,* Geffen,1986.

Bill Frisell
Have a Little Faith, Nonesuch, 1993.

Also see John Scofield.

Go West: Music for the Films of Buster Keaton, Nonesuch, 1995.

In Line, ECM, 1983.

Howard Alden
Take Your Pick, Concord Jazz, 1997.

Encore!, Live at Centre Concorde, Concord Jazz, 1995. Co-led by Ken Peplowski, a reeds player.

Alden has many albums available, all of them recommended.

Howard Alden/George Van Eps
Seven and Seven, Concord, 1993.

Ron Affif
Ringside, Pablo, 1997.

52nd Street, Pablo, 1996.

Emily Remler
East to Wes, Concord, 1988. Especially notable for her work with pianist Hank Jones. Emily recorded many other records for Concord in the 1980s. *See also* Larry Coryell.

John Pizzarelli, Jr.
New Standards, Novus, 1994. Includes the tune "Beautiful Moons Ago," written by Oscar Moore.

Naturally, Novus, 1993.

Pizzarelli has many albums available.

Peter Bernstein
Brain Dance, Criss Cross, 1997.

Lou Donaldson's Caracas, Milestone, 1994.

Russell Malone
Russell Malone, Columbia, 1992.

Black Butterfly, Columbia, 1993.

Diana Krall's Love Scenes, Impulse, 1997.

Roy Hargrove's Habana, Verve, 1997. With the group Crisol.

Mark Whitfield
Forever Love, Verve, 1997.

Sonny Sharrock and Derek Bailey
Sharrock and Bailey are two free and abstract jazz guitarists, who have been dealt with only in passing in this book. They are nevertheless part of the fascinating modern history of jazz guitar. Sonny Sharrock, *Ask the Ages,* Axiom Records, 1991.

Derek Bailey, *The Last Wave,* DIW (an import), 1996.

Derek Bailey, Pat Metheny, Gregg Bendian, and Paul Wertico, *The Sign of 4,* Knitting Factory Works, 1997. A free, avant-garde, or abstract jazz recording.

Other Albums to Note
Ed Bickert's duo with pianist Bill Mays, *Concord Duo Series, Vol. 7,* Concord Jazz, 1994. Bickert is a superb Canadian guitarist who rarely plays in the United States.

Guitarists Tommy Bolin and John Tropea on Billy Cobham's *Spectrum,* Rhino Records, 1973. Also of interest are recordings by Larry Carlton and all the Brazilians.

A note about recording studio players: Not included in this book but of special interest are Tommy Tedesco, primarily known as a studio player on the West Coast. He is one of the most recorded guitar players in the world and worked in the Doc Severinson orchestra; Vince Bell, an East Coast studio player on many albums; and studio players John Tropea, a versatile guitarist, and Grant Geissman, who played, among many other tunes, the song "Feels So Good" on the hit recording by Chuck Mangione.

For More Information

Books

Alkyer, Frank, editor, *Downbeat—60 Years of Jazz* (Milwaukee: Hal Leonard Corporation, 1995).

Balliett, Whitney, *American Musicians: 56 Portraits in Jazz* (New York: Oxford University Press, 1986). This book contains a very informative chapter on guitarist Jim Hall.

Bruynoghe, Yannick, *Big Bill Blues* (London: Cassell and Company, 1955).

Charters, Samuel, *The Country Blues* (New York: Rinehart, 1975)

Crow, Bill, *From Birdland to Broadway* (New York: Oxford University Press, 1992). This book contains anecdotes about many musicians, including the guitarists. Pages 220 to 227, for example, have tales about Eddie Condon, Attila Zoller, and Joe Puma.

Dance, Helen Oakley, *Stormy Monday: The T-Bone Walker Story* (Baton Rouge and New York: Louisiana State University Press and Da Capo Press, 1987).

Delaunay, Charles, *Django Reinhardt* (New York: Da Capo Press, 1961).

Evans, Roger, *How to Play Guitar* (New York: St. Martin's Press, 1979). This thorough book takes would-be guitarists from the first steps, from choosing a guitar, to first attempts to practice, to advanced performance. It is one of many such books on the market, and while it leaves no doubt about the complexity of the task of learning to play the guitar, it also prevents a student from floundering.

Feather, Leonard, *Inside Jazz* (New York: Da Capo, 1977). Originally published as *Inside Bebop* (New York: J. J. Robbins,1949). This book, about the beboppers, has material on such guitarists as Irving Ashby, Billy Bauer, Charlie Christian, Bill de Aranjo, Barney Kessel, Remo Palmier, and Chuck Wayne.

———, *The Passion for Jazz* (New York: Horizon Press, 1980). This book has a chapter on Pat Metheny.

Giddins, Gary, *Rhythm-a-ning—Jazz Tradition and Innovation in the '80s* (New York: Oxford University Press, 1985).

Gillespie, Dizzy, with Al Fraser, *To Be or Not to Bop* (New York: Doubleday, 1979). This important and fascinating book, which documents the bebop era, is easy to read and understand, and it includes all the musicians that passed through Dizzy's life, including guitarist Charlie Christian.

Hadlock, Richard, *Jazz Masters of the 20s* (New York: Macmillan, 1972). This book has important chapters on Eddie Lang and the Chicagoans; the latter includes guitarist Eddie Condon in recounting the history of jazz in Chicago in the 1920s and 1930s.

Hall, Jim, *Exploring Jazz Guitar* (Miwaukee: Hal Leonard, 1990). This book contains Jim Hall's personal approach to all aspects of guitar playing, from performing to preparing for performances and record dates to constructions of solos, with sheet music examples illustrating many of his explanations.

Hentoff, Hal, *Listen to the Stories* (New York: HarperCollins, 1995). This book has chapters on guitarists Danny Barker, Eddie Condon, and Herb Ellis, with mentions of many others.

Kernfeld, Barry, editor, *The New Grove Dictionary of Jazz* (New York: Grove's Dictionaries of Music, 1995).

Lees, Gene, *Oscar Peterson: The Will to Swing* (Rocklin, CA: Prima, 1990). This book has material on many guitarists who played with the Oscar Peterson Trio, particularly Herb Ellis.

Maggin, Donald L., *Stan Getz: A Life in Jazz* (New York: Morrow, 1996).

Menn, Don, editor, *Secrets from the Masters — Conversations with Forty Great Guitar Players* (San Francisco: GPI Books, Miller Freeman, 1992).

Sallis, James, editor, *The Guitar in Jazz* (Lincoln: University of Nebraska Press, 1996).

Shapiro, Nat, and Nat Hentoff, editors, *The Jazz Makers — Essays on the Greats of Jazz* (New York: Rinehart, 1957).

Shaughnessy, Mary Alice, *Les Paul: An American Original* (New York: Morrow, 1992).

Simon, George T., *The Big Bands* (New York: Schirmer Books, 1981). This authoritative and easy-to-read reference book thoroughly explores the music of the swing era in general, all the bands, and many important musicians, including quite a few of the guitarists discussed in this book.

Summerfield, Maurice J., *The Jazz Guitar, third edition* (Newcastle Upon Tyne, UK: Ashley Mark, 1993). Note: This company has published many books about guitars and guitarists.

Periodicals

Magazines on guitar playing of all types—from country and western to blues to pop, rock and roll, rhythm and blues, and jazz—outnumber all other music magazines. Among the best known are *Guitar* and *Guitar Player*. Magazines covering the jazz field in general often focus on guitar players and sometimes devote entire issues to guitars. Among them are *Down Beat*, *Jazz Times*, *Jazz Iz*, foreign publications in the English language such as the *British Jazz Journal* and the *Canadian Jazz Report*, and a little magazine published in New York state called *Cadence* (Cadence Building, Redwood, New York 13679; phone 315-287-2852).

For example, in May 1990, *Jazz Times* magazine published a special guitar issue covering such players as Stanley Jordan, Larry Coryell, Kenny Burrell, J. J. Cale, Robben Ford, Frank Gambale, Steve Khan, John McLaughlin, and Lee Ritenour. Another issue of *Jazz Times*, in August 1994, was devoted to jazz guitarists and included profiles of Jim Hall, Mike Stern, Toninho Horta of Brazil, Peter Leitch, Frank Gambale, as well as a survey of jazz guitar recordings by John Abercrombie, Howard Alden, Charlie Byrd, Larry Coryell, Sonny Sharrock, Scott Henderson, Peter Leitch, Lee Ritenour, John Scofield, Tal Farlow, John Stowell, and other articles and items focusing on guitarists, including an obituary of Joe Pass, who had just died at the age of 65. To obtain these and other back issues, write to the magazine.

Jazz Times
8737 Colesville Road, 5th floor
Silver Spring, Maryland 20910-3921
Phone 301-588-4114
Fax 301-588-2009

For back issues of *Down Beat*, write to that magazine:
102 North Haven Road
Elmhurst, Illinois 60126-2970
Phone 630-941-2030
Fax 630-941-3210

For back issues of *Jazz Iz*, write to that magazine:
3620 N.W. 43rd Street
Gainesville, Florida 32606-8103
Phone 352-375-3705
Fax 352-375-7268

In New York City, a little monthly magazine called *Hot House* is distributed free of charge in jazz clubs and contains listings of all the players in the region's club for the month, plus at least two profiles of musicians appearing in town that month. Articles have appeared on hundreds of musicians: for example, guitarists Russell Malone in the October 1997 issue; Vic Juris in February 1997; Al Dimeola in November 1996; Tal Farlow in June 1996; Kevin Eubanks in August 1995; Joe Diorio in December 1995; Mark Whitfield in October 1994; Peter Bernstein in March 1994; John Scofield in November 1993; John McLaughlin in April 1992; Mary Osborne in August 1991; and Jim Hall in April 1989. For back issues, which may be available for a small charge, write:

Gene Kalbacher, editor and publisher
18 Whippoorwill Lane
Rockaway Township, New Jersey 07866
Phone 201-627-5349.

Another recommended magazine is *Just Jazz Guitar*, available by subscription only:
P.O. Box 76053
Atlanta, Georgia 30358-1053

Internet Sites

Jazz 52nd Street

http://www.52ndstreet.com/
The Internet's largest CD jazz review site contains more than eight hundred reviews.

Jazz Central Station

http://www.jazzcentralstation.com
Includes dates of upcoming jazz concerts and festivals, as well as a wide range of jazz-related information.

Jazz Corner

http://www.jazzcorner.com/index.html
Features information about musicians and organizations, concerts and club dates, the business of jazz, and a chat room.

Jazz Guitar OnLine

http://www.jazzguitar.com
An online magazine that features articles about jazz guitarists and performances. Also includes classified ads and jazz news.

Jazz Institute of Chicago

http://www.JazzInstituteOfChicago.org/
Numerous articles on jazz personalities and histories, as well as a performance calendar.

Jazz Online

http://www.jazzonln.com/
A central site for reviews, interviews, and news; includes a vast database of audio and video clips of contemporary jazz musicians.

Just Jazz Guitar

http://rampages.onramp.net/~jazzgtr./jjg.html
A website sponsored by the print magazine of the same name. Features articles, photos, and links.

To learn more about individual artists, visit the following sites:

Larry Coryell

http:stange.simplenet.com/coryell

Peter Leitch

http://www.jazzcorner.com/leitch.html

Pat Martino

http://patmartino.com

John McLaughlin

http://www.acns.nwu.edu/jazz/artists/mclaughlin.john

Wes Montgomery

http://www.glolink.com/WES

John Scofield

http://www.c-and-c.si/sco/index.html

Index

Numbers in *italics* indicate illustrations.

About the Author

Leslie Gourse has researched and written stories for various mediums, including CBS, *The New York Times*, *The Los Angeles Times*, and *The Boston Globe*. Her articles have appeared in magazines and newspapers, covering general culture, social trends, and music. Her books, including *Dizzy Gillespie and the Birth of Bebop* and *The Triumph and Tragedy of Lady Day*, have earned high praise from the critics. For Franklin Watts, Ms. Gourse is the author of the entire Art of Jazz series, including these titles: *Blowing on the Changes: The Art of the Jazz Horn Players*; *Deep Down in Music: The Art of the Great Jazz Bassists*; *Striders to Beboppers and Beyond: The Art of the Jazz Piano*; *Swingers and Crooners: The Art of Jazz Singing*; and *Timekeepers: The Great Jazz Drummers*.